EDITORIAL

Feminist Review has been publishing regularly since 1979. Conceived in a period of optimism about feminism and socialism, and the possibilities for socialist feminism, the journal from the outset included inter-national issues and debates around class, alongside the more expected women's studies themes.

Feminist Review 17 (1984) was a clear indicator that 'race' was a problem for *FR* – both in the journal and for the collective of women working voluntarily to bring it out. Black women had been organizing together for a long time, formulating and expressing criticisms of white-dominated feminisms. *FR* was aware of these challenges, and yet the collective remained one comprised of all white women. *FR* 17 was a Black feminist issue, given over to an autonomous group of Black feminists – the first and last time for such a departure from general *FR* practice.

Much has changed since 1984. A small number of Black women have joined the collective. The will of the collective to represent Black women, questions around racism and race have sharpened, but not unproblematically – who could believe otherwise! In issue 36, *FR* editorialized its desire to publish more of such writing. Looking back from 1992 you can see challenging articles by Black and ethnic-minority women on various issues around race, identity and feminism. However, while the journal provided a place for these ideas and debates, in many respects the collective remained outside the political and cultural moment from which they arose.

Feminism had itself changed radically; it had become more self-conscious and stronger in spirit through the recognition that it was not a single voice. The diversity and difference of women's lives upon which Black feminists had so long insisted – once acknowledged – changed the political and theoretical shape of feminism. The old feminism was, as many know well, no stranger to division: but it was a division unified by the shared political rhetoric of the grand narrative and utopian transformation. Initially moulded by these political senti-ments, *FR* debated their limitations and gave voice to the growing

disenchantment with such world-views. But for the collective the
political import of the new language of difference and diversity proved a
rather more difficult adjustment. Part of the collective's identity
remained within the old feminism and it proved – for many different
reasons – both difficult to see, and difficult to surrender.

This ambivalence around the changing ground of feminism generated its own malaise: the work of the collective in producing the journal
became strained and routinized, often proceeding on automatic pilot
according to a largely assumed and unspoken political agenda. Thus,
paradoxically, while the journal increasingly carried pieces on the
changing, more self-conscious, positioned and reflexive terrain of
feminist theory and politics, the collective became more functional and
pragmatic. Within these limiting circumstances, however, debate
continued, as did the commitment to change the identity of the
collective.

FR's attempt to broaden Black women's participation in the *FR*
project foundered in 1990. Three Black women out of five on the
collective left in sorrow in the spring, frustrated by the collective's lack
of will in taking up particular political points they had individually, and
finally collectively, brought up. Their intervention problematized the
practice and politics of the collective and inspired a sustained confrontation with what had been, until then, a set of working assumptions
about our openness as a collective, and about precisely what was
entailed in our commitment to antiracism. Like all assumptions, closer
examination revealed a diversity of views and understandings and this
fragmentation proved a difficult starting point from which to reconsider
the issue of race, and why we yet remained a predominantly white
collective. The questions were, of course, intimately linked but it was
only through the enforced recognition of our own 'otherness' that the
links became apparent.

The process of 'putting our house in order' was also a process of
leaving the home of old feminism. Although it had become somewhat
uncomfortable, it retained some of the certainties of earlier struggles.
As well, however, it represented the sediment of accumulated and
unresolved dilemmas of academics vs. activists, of élitism, exclusion and
marginalization of the outsider. These problems of power, hierarchy and
hidden agendas are no strangers to political collectives. Nor are they
ones to which there is 'a solution'. However, to the extent that they begin
to operate through the collective unconscious they certainly become – to
continue the earlier metaphor – a corrosive foundation. It was to these
problems the Black women pointed in finally registering their inability
to remain within the collective. What had been, effectively, a strategy
for limited survival as a collective was shown to be unviable, particularly and especially if that strategy was concerned to open up the journal
to Black, Third World, and ethnic minority women, and to participate in
the struggles against racism.

We had duplicated yet another of 'nature's' couplets. In much the
same way as issues around sexuality fell to the lesbian women on the
collective, politics to the activists, the family to the heterosexuals, and

expertise to the experts, etc., we had attempted to deal with the issue of 'race' and the homogeneity of the collective by bringing in more Black women. Black women were taken to represent, first and foremost, an antiracist politics, a compartmentalization which, like all the others, both set up false categories and boundaries, and located the problem as 'other' in the sense that it became the provenance of a specific group rather than the collective as a whole. Moreover, it constituted a negation of who and what Black, ethnic minority, and Third World women are and represent, in much the same way as labels such as 'lesbian', 'activist', and 'heterosexual' are such poor refractions of both individual and collective identity. The difference and diversity that has been foregrounded by contemporary (including Black) feminism is not about a pluralistic or pluralized tolerance of categories of difference. These concepts address the hierarchies and exclusions which make up the social relationships of race, sexuality, class and gender which intersect in constructing historical identity and political realities. These relationships mutually and similarly connect 'white' and 'black' women first and foremost in the language, politics and reality of racism. Those Black women who left the collective did so in part because their political participation was impossible as long as only one side of that equation was recognized.

Now *FR* is faced at the beginning of the 1990s with a situation it is determined to meet and negotiate carefully – and hopefully with some success. The content of the journal, while by no means perfect, has changed significantly. The collective has begun a process of changing our working practices in an attempt to reach beyond the networks within which we have worked traditionally, to bring in not only Black and Third World women and the range of areas of work and politics in which they are involved, but also other women whose voices have not been heard in the pages of the journal. We want to make *Feminist Review* a place where women of many different ethnic origins would want to work – as collective members as well as writers.

We hope to encourage more critical thought and reflection on all the political vocabularies and strategies which as feminists we engage in, even as we are using those vocabularies in our workplaces and in our everyday living and thinking. Political labels are crude and limited ways of representing our political identities but they are also necessary. So, too, are categories such as race which we perforce must use even as we recognize there are no such thing as 'races'. We would therefore especially welcome articles which help to sharpen our understanding of the different ways in which we speak of race and its relation to gender – 'race' itself, questions of ethnicity and nationality, the different forms of xenophobia and ethnocentrisms, the histories of racialist knowledges and practices, and the questions of identity and subjectivity. These are all areas we need to explore further, both as a way of deconstructing the self-evident language of race and racism, and constructing an analytical and political language with which to appreciate difference and diversity.

Also, we hope the journal will become a platform for rethinking the vocabularies of socialism and class. These issues are also, for *FR*, important elements in the differentiated feminist project. Issue 39 gave some indication of the immensely contradictory flux which is shaping the lives of women in the Soviet Union and Eastern Europe. It also acknowledged the lacunae in political thought created by the crisis of socialism and the difficulty this poses for those of us who wish to signal that the world can be a better place. It is not just the communist world which is undergoing transformation. The changes which continue to motivate globalization are ones which map the engendered international division of labour in starker and starker terms. The intersecting lines of class and gender so often used to draw the boundaries of nationalism are increasingly racialized to accommodate international realignments. In Western Europe, the language of citizenship systematically articulates the status of the outsider, and subjects 'migrant' women to more intensive and extensive exploitation. All of these extraordinary changes demand a reconsideration of political and theoretical frameworks as well as a new feminist vision of the future. Hopefully, *FR* will provide a platform for these important questions and help foster a new feminist imagination.

In anticipation of this, we are trying to make criteria for articles both more explicit and more responsive to the many idioms of feminist thinking, expression and politics. In this process we think we have begun to dislodge the old assumptions and their attendant frailties and, although it has been difficult and taken up many hours of testing consideration, it has generated resolve, energy and enthusiasm for the new but ongoing *FR* project. Although much, of necessity, remains unresolved, we hope the journal and the collective will grasp the nettle of uncertainty and ambiguity and engage with the conditions and strategies of women's lives and our aspirations for change.

As part of this process the collective has also, of course, debated the question of *FR* taking on an antiracist policy. It was recognized that to do so would not be without difficulty. There was concern that it would invoke some of the problematic ethos generated by earlier antiracist politics, whereas what we wanted to do was build on the strength created by that political intervention. As well, we wanted to draw on the strength of the antiracist tradition that stretches beyond our more immediate political past in which 'antiracist' politics were so influential. However, there was concern too that if we invoked that more recent 'antiracist' tradition such a statement could fall into the trap of formalism and closure, inspiring new patterns of exclusion. 'Antiracist' politics arose at a particular historical juncture and have enabled both Black and white involvement in an active opposition to racism. But is it enough? What are the politics of antiracism? What gets built on them?

These questions continue to preoccupy collective discussion and debate. Finally, however, they were thought not to be reasons against adopting such a policy, but rather difficulties to be aware of so as not to undermine or abort our collective commitment to the continuing struggles against racism. In that spirit, *FR* hopes to draw from the years of experience, the work of Black feminists, and the critical analyses of Black activists and take the challenge of racism further through the changing language and politics of antiracism. Our respect for the achievements of earlier antiracist policies co-exists with a recognition of the need to be part of a politics and analyses which articulate difference, take on contradictions and ambiguity, avoid moralism and nurture radicalism. It is in this spirit we wish to express our commitment as an antiracist journal. It is made at a time when the hideousness and ubiquity of racism and its impact on the lives of women (and men) cannot be doubted.

As a journal, *Feminist Review* wants to challenge the racist discourses that increasingly pervade our globalized world. We hope to provide analyses of the realignments of power that fuel ethnic conflicts and which continue to racialize minority groups. We want to continue the work analyzing and confronting racist representations of women, and the deepening and entrenched intersections of race, gender, class and sexuality. We hope, too, that the journal can contribute to creating languages and structures of feeling which will encourage new forms of political organization and activity.

The collective also want the journal to continue to explore the different strands of antiracism within the women's movement. To reflect on the attempts to undermine institutionalized racism; to review the successes of recent 'racism awareness' campaigns; the attempts to radicalize equal opportunities programmes, and to confront institutionalized racism in women's organizations. The journal also wants to carry articles on the question of cultural or religious separatism, of identity politics and the political options open to feminists within and without such boundaries. It also wishes to publish articles analyzing cultural politics – the arenas of creativity and artistic practice – within the communities of Black and ethnic-minority women. It hopes to give much greater voice to the historical and cross-cultural work being done which is providing a more detailed mapping of our political realities as always imbricated by race, gender, sexuality and class. The journal wants to participate in and contribute to the discussions, debates and political networks which are shaping and examining these issues. In making such a statement, we recognize that we are, as a collective, initiating a process rather than presenting something cast in tablets of stone. What we hope we have indicated here is our commitment to political change in opening up the journal to all the discussions and issues that make up the diversity of feminism. We anticipate and welcome your contributions and support.

FLEURS DU MAL OR SECOND-HAND ROSES?:Natalie Barney, Romaine Brooks, and the 'Originality of the Avant-Garde'

Bridget Elliott and Jo-Ann Wallace

The notion of a modernist avant-garde has proven troublesome in much recent feminist writing. For a start, as Susan Suleiman points out, the term is annoyingly imprecise and even slightly ridiculous:

> To say the word 'avant-garde' today is to risk falling into a conceptual and terminological quagmire. Is 'avant-garde' synonymous with, or to be subtly distinguished from, the experimental, the bohemian, the modern, the modern*ist*, the postmodern? Is it a historical category or a transhistorical one? A purely aesthetic category or a philosophical/ political/existential one? Is it still to be taken seriously, or does it 'conjure up comical associations of aging youth'? In short, does the word have specific content or has it become so vague and general as to be virtually useless? (Suleiman, 1988: 148)

Equally disturbing is the conspicuous shortage of women writers and artists who have been classified as avant-garde in the standard literary and art historical surveys of the early twentieth century. Even though women have traditionally occupied marginal spaces in patriarchal culture, it seems that (despite a few exceptional exceptions, like Gertrude Stein and Meret Oppenheim) they have frequented the wrong margins. Instead of appearing as strikingly original and fashionably vanguard, the work of women writers and artists has, more often than not, been described as derivative, deviant, old-fashioned, and second-rate. Evidently, mainstream bourgeois culture draws important distinctions between those privileged outsiders who are recognized as daringly advanced and a whole host of insignificant 'others' whose differences are simply uninteresting.

In this article we want to address two issues. The first is the question of how differences are constituted as significant in the avant-garde discourses of twentieth-century culture. One of the most important mechanisms for differentiating between *and evaluating* various forms of deviance and marginality has been the binary opposition of original/copy. This opposition, more often than not, has marked the difference between masculine and feminine creative work in critical reconstructions of avant-garde modernism. However, the valorizing of 'originality' in avant-garde discourse – neatly summed up in Ezra Pound's exhortation to 'make it new' – is also conflated with a celebration of 'the difficult', and little critical attention has been paid to the political and social effectiveness of such strategies. One ironic consequence of this is that although 'the margins' continue to be celebrated as feminine spaces, the women who inhabit them remain insignificant unless they accept an individualist ethos and produce recognizably 'original' work.[1] The second issue we want to address is the question of why so many early modernist women resurrected the literary and visual styles of the Decadents, Symbolists, and Aesthetes of the late nineteenth century. We will suggest that while this 'borrowing' or 'echoing' of earlier styles has led to a critical devaluation of their work as derivative and second-rate, its strategic importance can only be understood within the context of an emerging discourse surrounding feminine, and especially lesbian sexuality.

We will explore these issues by focusing on the work and critical reception of two women active during the first three decades of this century: writer and salonist Natalie Clifford Barney and painter Romaine Brooks. We want to challenge the avant-garde's limited definition of originality, and the structures of cultural author-ity it (en)genders, by looking at the ways in which Barney and Brooks have been constructed as 'second-hand' artists in three overlapping areas: their art has been seen as of only secondary interest to their lives; they have been described as working in 'old-fashioned' genres; and their lesbian sexuality (particularly that of cross-dresser Brooks), which formed the basis of much of their artistic production, was regarded as a pale copy of heterosexual norms. We are not interested here in evaluating their work or in arguing that it should be included in avant-garde literary or art historical canons. Rather, we want to reconstruct *their* reasons for making the artistic choices they did. To do this, we will focus on work which was produced in Paris during a period of interdisciplinary collaboration between 1915 and 1929, or from the beginning of their relationship as lovers until a number of mutually inspired projects were completed. Of particular interest are Barney's *Poems & Poèmes: autres alliances* published in 1920, and several of Romaine Brooks's portraits exhibited in 1925.[2] Our study is cross-disciplinary in part because we want to avoid the fetishizing of formal devices that often occurs when media are treated in isolation. Instead, we want to take up broader institutional problems relating to critical evaluation and canonization that have plagued the disciplines of literary studies and art history in surprisingly similar ways. Further-more, the fact that most women were intrigued by representing themselves and their friends (who were similarly engaged in creative cultural pursuits such as dance, writing or the visual arts) reveals much about how they imag(in)ed their position – an imag(in)ing which sometimes bears little resemblance to their subsequent positioning in literary and art historical criticism.

In keeping with our thesis, our subtitle is, in part, *borrowed* from a 1981 essay by Rosalind E. Krauss. In 'The originality of the avant-garde', Krauss points to the fact that '[o]ne thing only seems to hold fairly constant in the vanguardist discourse and that is the theme of originality'; she then notes the ways in which the notion of 'originality' is bound together in a kind of aesthetic economy with a notion of repetition; and, finally, she deconstructs the 'originality/repetition' binary, concluding that both the avant-garde and modernism *'depend on'* (our emphasis) a repression of the second term of that binary code. While Krauss's essay grounds our own analysis of the critical reception of such artists as Barney and Brooks, we want to further her argument by considering two related issues which she does not discuss: the ways in which the second term of that binary has been feminized, and the ways in which the avant-garde – and especially the modernist avant-garde – has been consistently constructed in the masculine.

Feminist developments in translation theory provide a useful paradigm for unsettling the 'original/repetition' binary and thus en-abling a rereading of work formerly regarded as *only* derivative and therefore second-rate. In this section we will trace the evolution of recent translation theory moving from conceptualizations of translation as a 'feminine' to a 'feminist' activity. Much of this work builds on George Steiner's *After Babel: Aspects of Language and Translation* (1975). There Steiner describes almost any act of interpretation as a kind of translation, emphasizing that translation occurs not only between languages (or disciplines) but within them (Steiner, 1975: 28). What Steiner calls 'internal translation' has both diachronic and synchronic dimensions; we translate across time – as when we interpret an historical text or image – and across geographical *and cultural* spaces. Class, race, age and gender all map and speak from within different 'ideolects' (Steiner, 1975: 46).

Significantly, Steiner sexualizes and feminizes the act of interpre-tation as well as the figure of the interpreter or translator: 'There is a strain of femininity in the great interpreter, a submission, made active by intensity of response, to the creative presence' (Steiner, 1975: 26). Steiner describes the act of interpretation or translation as essentially passive – the translator *responds to* but does not initiate or originate – and therefore feminine. While Steiner suggests that translation is an innately feminine activity, Lori Chamberlain traces the ways in which translation has been culturally constructed as 'derivative' *and thus* feminine, as opposed to authorship which is 'original' and thus masculine. Authorship is overdetermined as a relation of production and therefore of an engendering authority, while translation is a relation of re-production and therefore of a corresponding lack of authority. In her discussion of the 'sexualization' of translation metaphors, Chamberlain argues that:

> The cultural elaboration of this view suggests that in the original abides what is natural, truthful, and lawful, in the copy, what is artificial, false and treasonous. Translations can be, for example, echoes (in musical terms), copies or portraits (in painterly terms), or borrowed or ill-fitting clothes (in sartorial terms). (1988: 455)

The denigration of the copyist has been explored in the visual arts by Linda Nochlin who points out that realism is falsely perceived by its detractors as 'a "discovery" of preexisting objects out there or a simple "translation" of ready-made reality into art' (Nochlin, 1973: 25). Here the notion of copyist refers not only to the realist who directly transcribes nature but also to the practice of copying masterpieces, an activity that was especially important before the advent of photographic reproduction. Although copyists were often highly skilled specialists, their lack of originality meant that they were regarded as a lower order of artist (see Duro, 1986 and 1988). This denigration of realism appears in Roger Fry's foundational modernist criticism where a dichotomy is set up between 'fidelity to appearance' and the more highly valued 'purely aesthetic criteria' (see Fry, 1981: 8–9; and Nochlin, 1973: 37–8). According to Fry, the purer art becomes, the less it can be related to the material world, which in turn leads to the increasing rarification of its audience. Although Nochlin explores the class biases of a modernist position that rejects the mundane world of the masses, she does not consider its gender implications.

However, many feminists have also drawn on a translation metaphor to describe the positioning of women in patriarchal culture, suggesting that women are 'always already' bilingual and bicultural, translating our experiences into and out of the codes and systems of men. This approach, which has evolved from deconstructionist and semiotic theories of intertextuality, has necessitated rethinking every text as a translation (see Spivak, 1976: xiii; Eagleton, 1977). Since all writing (or painting, for that matter) enters a system in which it is understood relationally, no single work can be seen as original. Barbara Godard develops these ideas with respect to explicitly feminist discourse which she sees functioning as translation in two rather different ways: it can make visible or audible 'what has been hitherto "unheard of"', and it can self-consciously re-write, imitate, mimic and thus convert dominant discourses. Godard thus enlarges the concept of translation to 'include imitation, adaption, quotation, pastiche, parody – all different modes of re-writing: in short all forms of interpenetration of works and discourses' (Godard, 1989: p. 50).

Significantly, however, the avant-garde canons in literature and the visual arts privilege originality despite the slippery ways in which that term has been defined.[3] In our opening quote, Suleiman's list of shifting criteria for avant-garde identity – including the experimental, bohemian, modern, modern*ist*, and postmodern – is organized around such diverse issues as the form and content of the work, the lifestyle of the artist, and categories of artistic criticism. To qualify as avant-garde, is it necessary to be perceived as radical in all these respects? Or are some more important than others? And is it problematic to conceptualize these categories separately given their common strongly individualist bias which takes the form of a willingness to experiment with representational conventions and lifestyles?

The two models of translation sketched above – as derivative and thus feminine, or as appropriative, engaged, *re-productive* and thus feminist – can serve as different models for understanding the projects of Natalie Clifford Barney and Romaine Brooks. For the most part, critics and scholars have uncritically employed the feminine paradigm when assessing their art and lives. To varying degrees, both have been cast as derivative *and therefore* second-rate artists: Barney as influenced to too great an extent by such Decadent poets as Baudelaire, and Brooks as having swallowed whole the palette of Whistler. Certainly, the continuing undervaluing of Barney and Brooks even in reconstituted feminist literary and art historical canons indicates the degree to which as feminists we have been unable to disentangle ourselves from the binary oppositions which structure our cultural experience. We are left wondering whether or not we too have overinvested in the concepts of 'originality' and 'genius'. Certainly, as feminists of the 1990s interpreting or translating the work of Natalie Barney and Romaine Brooks, we must be sensitive to both the historical and cultural contexts from which they spoke. But we must also be sensitive to the ways in which they were themselves engaged in acts of translation, interpretation and appropriation. We must take into account all of the resonances and residues that are left behind as their texts and images move across time and space.

One of the most interesting aspects of the scanty literature on Barney and Brooks is the fact that their creative works have been virtually devoured by their lives. Shari Benstock has recently commented on this problem in Barney's case:

> To date, Natalie Barney's life has been rendered as gossip – lesbian gossip rather than literary gossip. Her work remains unread, most of it untranslated, and her autobiography has not yet been published. Because her writing has not been taken seriously (if read at all, it is read as confirmation of her sexual and social exploits), commentaries on Barney have constituted remembrances by those who knew her or knew of her. (Benstock, 1986: 271–2).

And, although Brooks's work has received more sustained attention, her life has also loomed disproportionately large in critical assessments of her significance. It could be argued that this is the negative side of having a life that 'had the makings of legend'[4]. We know the intricate details of Barney's and Brooks's fabulous fortunes, scandalous love affairs, outrageous dress, and even their interior furnishings, all of which figured prominently in a number of novels by their contemporaries.[5] For instance, Barney appears in Liane de Pougy's *Idylle saphique* (1901), Radclyffe Hall's *The Well of Loneliness* (1928), and Lucie Delarue-Mardrus's *L'Ange et les pervers* (1930), while Brooks appears in Radclyffe Hall's *Adam's Breed* (1926) and Compton Mackenzie's *Extraordinary Women* (1928). Significantly, the same sort of sensational treatment continues in more recent biographies such as Jean Chalon's *Portrait of a Seductress: The World of Natalie Barney* (1976) and Meryle Secrest's *Between Me and Life: A Biography of Romaine Brooks* (1974) which at times exhibit an almost tabloid-style voyeurism. Repeatedly it is their lives (as opposed to their works) which are constructed as enduring artifacts – a strategy which is made clear in the following review of a 1962 special issue of *Adam* devoted to Natalie Barney:

> On the whole . . . I am not inclined to think that we have neglected an important writer though I shall hurry to obtain 'Souvenirs Indiscrets', but I do feel that we are neglecting an important human being, trailing clouds of glory from the golden age of Les Annees Dix, of the Mercure and the N.R.F., of Proust and Apollinaire, Cubism and Les Six, and with an exceptional gift of friendship. (Connolly, undated)

Ironically, the aestheticizing of Barney's and Brooks's lives – the cult of personality which pervades their biographies – seems to have lowered rather than raised the value of their creative work, perhaps because their conflation of art and life runs counter to the 'kind of Platonism' espoused by modernist critics wherein 'that which is removed from actuality is, by definition, the most aesthetically valuable' (Nochlin, 1973: 40). In contrast, the social embeddedness of Brooks's painting and Barney's writing has been seen as allowing *unproblematic* access to their personal histories and to their historical and cultural milieux. That is, their lives have been deemed of greater interest than their art. While a cult of personality has to some degree arisen around many male modernists – Ernest Hemingway and Pablo Picasso are obvious examples – the individualism of the male artist, his tragic or heroic originality, and, frequently, his self-sacrifice to his art are emphasized as salient features of avant-gardism. This emphasis on male originality seems curiously unwarranted given that the economically self-supporting, markedly heterosexual lifestyles of Hemingway and Picasso were more characteristic of the dominant bourgeois culture of the period than Barney's or Brooks's inherited fortunes and highly visible lesbianism. It would seem that Barney's and Brooks's class privileges and frequently conservative politics have disconcerted mainstream academics and feminist scholars alike – perhaps because both groups have predominantly middle-class allegiances. To some extent, lingering antiaristocratic sentiments seem to have fostered the view that Barney and Brooks were amateurish dilettantes as opposed to serious professionals.

The confusion between Barney's and Brooks's art and lives would seem to have been reinforced by the fact that for both women personal traces were vital to their work; most of Barney's texts contain elements of autobiography and memoir, while the subjects of Brooks's portraits were herself and her friends. (Because she did not need to earn her livelihood, Brooks was able to choose her sitters, very carefully selecting only those whose physical appearance and personality interested her. (Breeskin, 1986: 23))[6] However, there is little evidence that their work was any more autobiographical than that of, for example, Hemingway or Picasso; the evidence suggests instead that Barney's and Brooks's work has been interpreted as *merely* and *transparently* personal.

The idea that a writer or artist is simply copying the material world or transcribing personal experience rests on two interrelated assumptions which have shaped traditional masculinist views of autobiography. These are a belief in the prior existence of a unified transcendent subject who can then unproblematically project himself in writing or painting. Celeste Schenck and Bella Brodzki have recently described this masculine tradition of autobiography as taking as its first premise 'the mirroring capacity of the autobiographer: *his* universality, *his* representativeness, *his* role as spokesman for the community'. In contrast, they suggest that the position of the female autobiographer necessitates a rather different framework: 'No mirror of *her* era, the female autobiographer takes as a given that selfhood is mediated; her invisibility results from her lack of a tradition, her marginality in a male-dominated culture, her fragmentation – social and political as well as psychic' (Schenck and Brodzki, 1988: 1).

This feminist critique of the autonomous self necessarily complicates our understanding of autobiographical writing which, instead of literally transcribing experience, involves the construction of self-images through the manipulation of pictorial or literary conventions. This fragmentation of the self has been much celebrated in recent feminist and postmodern writing about autobiography. Those women writers who consciously address the limits of the self have been more highly valued and central in the establishment of an alternative feminist canon. In this respect, Schenck and Brodzki's admiration of Gertrude Stein is typical when they describe her as providing 'the ultimate female autobiography – with a difference' (1988: 11). In their eyes, Stein's difference consists of her radically relational construction of female identity through her involvement with Alice Toklas. Stein is cast as pioneering the later radical autobiographical strategies of writers such as Roland Barthes, and praised for her '*refusal* to frame identity, conventionally and mimetically understood' (1988: 10).

While the construction of an alternative canon of 'female' autobiographical writing has enabled a new appreciation of many formerly marginalized writers, it has also tended to fetishize formal experimentation at the expense of other sorts of potentially radical practices. Romaine Brooks's still unpublished memoir, 'No pleasant memories', written in the 1930s, is one example. Although the veracity of this often fantastic autobiography has been questioned by several writers (e.g., Sir Harold Acton, who knew her in Rome, Norman Holmes Pearson, Carl Van Vechten, and Meryle Secrest), there has been little exploration of the ways in which Brooks borrowed liberally and self-consciously from Decadent and Symbolist iconography to construct herself as an outcast or *lapidée*. In this way, Brooks refused the invisibility of the woman artist and aggressively adopted the coherent marginality of an already outmoded masculine avant-garde. Significantly, despite some reservations about the accuracy of the autobiography, the art historical literature on Brooks has largely accepted her written self-representation and has failed to note similarities between her verbal and visual strategies.[7]

In some ways, the creation of an alternative 'female' canon (which sometimes seems to function as the binary opposite of traditional male practices) has led to a disconcertingly simplified framework. The case of Barney and Brooks highlights this problem in that their work seems to fall between these two standards of evaluation in its use of conventional genres which are often but not always turned to strikingly radical ends. Fitting into neither 'male' nor 'female' critical frameworks, the work of Barney and Brooks borrows from and messily exceeds each category, as we will explore below. Although the mismatch between Barney and Brooks and existing critical frameworks has led to them being denigrated as second-rate, the argument can be turned around to usefully highlight the short-comings of late twentieth-century criticism and its constructions of avant-garde modernism. In fact, when translated differently, the complexity and contradictions in the work of women like Barney and Brooks offer us just as many insights into women's complicated cultural positions as do the writings of, for example, Gertrude Stein.

A second recurring problem in critical evaluations of Barney and Brooks is the ways in which they are also seen, in their nonautobiographical work, as reviving conventional, even old-fashioned genres like the portrait and the courtly love poem. In taking up portraiture, Romaine Brooks was engaging a genre that was frequently perceived as derivative and commercially suspect. Throughout the eighteenth and nineteenth centuries, portraiture was held in relatively low esteem by academicians who tended to regard it as less imaginative and morally instructive than the more complicated genre of history painting, and by the emerging avant-garde who criticized it for all too often catering to conventional wealthy tastes – for selling the bourgeois suitably smug self-images.[8] Although portraiture was to some extent being rehabilitated in certain avant-garde sectors by artists like Picasso, such works were not the mainstay of these artists' production.

Romaine Brooks, *Self-Portrait* (1923). Oil on canvas. 117.5 × 68.3 cm. National Museum of American Art, Smithsonian Institution, gift of the artist.

And, in any case, unlike the bohemian Picasso, Brooks was an artist from the Right as opposed to the Left Bank. In other words, she was seen as part of an *haut monde* which preferred 'old-fashioned' Symbolist styles which invoked artists like Whistler, Condor, and Beardsley. For instance, the style of Brooks's *Self-Portrait* (1923) (Figure 1) bears a strong resemblance to such works as Charles Condor's *Portrait of Max Beerbohm* from the 1890s. The similarities extend well beyond the subdued tonalities and thinly painted surfaces of the background to include the presentation of stylishly poised figures in their immaculately tailored suits, identifying them as Society dandies. Brooks's limited palette of greys, black and white, her precise outlining and modelling, and her ethereally still atmospheric backgrounds deliberately resurrected a visual language of decadence, decay, and corruption which had been unfashionably *passé* (particularly in an English context) since the trial of Oscar Wilde. Brooks's preference for these forms (in contrast to more modernist Cubist fracturing, Fauve colouring, or Orphist celebrations of light and movement) has marked her out as imitative rather than innovative, an heir to old artistic wealth rather than the creator of new styles and schools.

The old-fashioned appearance of Brooks's portraits was not restricted to the style of her painting but also included her approach to composition and her use of conventions. For instance, in her painting of Natalie Barney as *L'Amazone* (1920) (Figure 2), the sitter is arranged in a time-honoured three-quarters pose and realistically rendered in terms of the details of her dress and her house, 20 rue Jacob, in the background, both of which indicate her wealthy status. Other accoutrements, such as the manuscript and miniature horse, make reference to Barney's passions for writing and riding. The horse additionally alludes to Barney's independence and to her famous and predominantly lesbian salon.[9] The fact that we are almost allegorically provided with so many insights into Barney's life establishes her as an independent entity who meets and returns the painter's gaze. Significantly, such autonomous sitters should be anathema to the modernist portrait painter, as Kirk Varnadoe indicates:

> [T]he modern artist is the giver, rather than the captor or preserver, of identity. The artist assigns to his subjects a particular expressiveness and significance that originates in his own work rather than in the personality he treats . . . The sitter is thus not simply placed in a referential system of accoutrements but more completely remade in terms of a system of artistic invention. . . .
>
> Since the modern portrait sitter acknowledges the artist's right to take liberties as he sees fit and accepts the artist's vision as valid on a level beyond comparable visual resemblance, the remaining *sine qua non* of the portrait, the indispensable element of identity, is the meaning conferred by the artist's stamp. Before being a banker or a critic or a poet, the modern sitter expects to become a Dubuffet, a Pearlstein, a de Kooning. (Columbia University, 1976: xiv–xv)

Romaine Brooks, *Natalie Barney 'L'Amazone'* (1920). Oil on canvas. 86.5 × 65.5 cm. © Musées de la Ville de Paris, 1991/VIS*ART Copyright Inc.

Clearly, Brooks did not assume the same sort of author-ity over her sitters as male modernist painters who were involved with projecting their perceptions on to a subject who was virtually 'swallowed up' (Columbia University, 1976: xviii). While the implication of Brooks's 'old-fashioned' approach will be considered in the next section, it is evident that it has disconcerted a number of modernist art historians, such as Joshua Taylor, who have resorted to special pleading for her recognition as a modernist:

> Romaine Brooks, in retaining contact with her own early preoccupation with character and the haunting loneliness of the individual was not being *retardataire*. By the 1920s her penetrating visual judgement could be seen as part of the new interest in psychology . . . If she were less of an individual, less truly aware of her own aloneness and the personal role art played in her life, she might be counted a surrealist or be fitted with some other useful title. But her modernity lies not in a pictorial method or a school, but in her tenacious adherence to the right to be herself, to fight her own psychic battles . . . (Breeskin, 1986: 18)

Here Brooks's traditional pictorial conventions are excused on the grounds that her modernism resides in her quest to explore her own tortured individuality through her art. In other words, she imposes her own emotional state rather than her style on her sitters. Of course, this interpretation is based upon an earlier Romantic conception of the artist wherein authenticity and sincerity become the most important kinds of truth (Battersby, 1990: 13).[10] As Adelyn Breeskin explains:

> Her own life was reflected in the people she depicted, and she has looked at both herself and her environment with a detachment that ill conceals the passion and imagination that were schooled in restraint by the cruelty of her early experience. (Breeskin, 1986: 19)

While this sort of special pleading argues that Brooks's portraits are not derivative in that she, the artist, is the real subject of the portrait, this viewing of Brooks through an older (i.e., pre-Modernist) Romantic paradigm once again conflates her art and life and implies that Brooks was translating her lived experience rather than creatively imagining new forms. Even the tough rhetoric of individualism cannot gloss over the fact that Brooks cannot be significantly original on these terms. A more creative re-reading of the original/copy opposition is needed.

In this respect it is perhaps more interesting to consider the ways in which gender differences informed the practice of portraiture. While Brooks's psychological interests may have seemed 'old-fashioned' as far as the painting of male subjects was concerned, it was a relatively new issue for female sitters and artists. As Deborah Silverman points out, it was only in the 1890s with the emergence of debates around the *femme nouvelle* that a new conception of portraying women as psychological subjects first emerged. Whereas men had previously been rendered in terms of their inner life and character, women had largely been depicted as decorative surfaces and fashions. According to Silverman, art critics such as Camille Mauclair and Marius-Ary Leblond began to notice how new conceptions of femininity might erode the older conventions for representing gender in portraiture (1989: 68–9). Since Mauclair's major essay on this subject was first published in 1899, it is evident that Brooks was involved with what was widely perceived as an experimental project as far as women were concerned. Clearly in this respect cultural agendas for men and women differed.

In much the same way that Brooks's portraiture drew upon an 'old-fashioned' genre, Natalie Barney drew upon the Symbolist poets and the courtly love tradition (as both Shari Benstock and Karla Jay have noted), adopting in many of her poems the voice of the male suitor: the page or the knight entreating the distant or cold lady.[11] Benstock suggests that 'the use of traditional [poetic] forms constituted an effort to summon literary authority, to place her poetry in a long and respected tradition' (Benstock, 1986: 240), while Jay similarly suggests that Barney 'sought to reclaim for women the whole of Western literary tradition from Sappho to the Symbolists' (Jay, 1988: 92). The need to summon authority by placing one's work in a recognized cultural tradition is a particularly pressing problem for women who have more often than not been exiled from prevailing literary and artistic canons. Frequently, a conflict arises between wanting to be taken seriously and legitimized as a writer or artist (which usually means working in either conventional or *recognizably* avant-garde forms) and a need to explore alternative forms and issues that relate to one's position as a woman. In the late nineteenth and early twentieth centuries these contradictory aspirations generated a schizophrenic notion of the relationship between gender and culture, as Celeste Schenck has observed:

> [W]omen are always subjected to competing stereotypes: they are both
> 'beneath' culture – too mired in nature to master the codes or poetic forms
> – and (notably in and after the Victorian period) 'upholders of' culture –
> hence rigid, conservative, form-bound, repressive of spontaneity and
> experimentation. The whole idea of the 'genteel' against which
> Modernism defined itself seems to be inextricably bound to these
> contradictory, even schizophrenic, notions of femininity. (Schenck,
> 1989: 228–9)

An interesting demonstration of these conflicting desires can be found in Natalie Barney's critical assessment, in her 1929 *Adventures de l'esprit*, of Romaine Brooks's painting. Throughout the text, Barney shifts uneasily between dismissing modernism, which she realizes is a framework that Brooks does not fit into, and championing Brooks's individuality in order to prove that she is a great artist and equal, if not superior, to her modernist contemporaries. Significantly, however, Barney locates Brooks's originality in her evocation of decadent sentiments. This is made clear in Barney's somewhat extravagant assertion that, en effet, Romaine Brooks n'appartient à aucun temps, à aucun pays, à aucun milieu, à aucune école, à aucune tradition; elle n'est pas non plus en révolution contre ces institutions, mais plutôt, comme Walt Whitman, ni pour ni contre elles – elle ne sait pas ce qu'elles sont. Elle est le résumé, la 'sommité fleurie' d'une civilisation à son déclin, dont elle a su recueillir la face. (Barney, 1929: 245)[12]

Taken at face value, Barney's text could simply be read as a statement of middle-aged, outmoded avant-gardism, the nostalgia of someone who had not kept up with changing aesthetic tastes and was still rooted in the decadent movement of her youth. This was certainly a charge made against her by Ezra Pound whom she hired in 1919 to advise her on the poems which would become the *Poems & Poèmes: autres alliances* volume. In his response to the manuscript, Pound stated that 'you are out of touch not only with editorial connections but with the best contemporary work' (Pound, 1976: 282). However, it can also be argued that Barney and her circle deliberately revived decadent modes for strategic as well as sentimental reasons. As we shall see, the strategic nature of this revival becomes apparent only if it is understood as part of a desire to make a newly emerging lesbian identity publicly visible.

The argument that Barney was simply summoning cultural authority by using the voice of, for example, the courtly love poet or the Wildean epigrammist firstly assumes an aesthetics of coherence that is completely absent from her *pensées* and her poetry, and secondly, ignores the transgressive effect of speaking in the masculine. It is also important to emphasize that in her poetry Barney was not speaking *as a man* but *in the literary voice of* a particular kind of male poet, one who was himself adopting either a conventional mask or a persona. In this way, Barney's poetic voice works in a way similar to – although by no means identical with – the transvestite costumes of Brooks and her sitters.

Barney practised a kind of poetics of the fragment, as one of her *pensées* – 'I never go to the end of an idea – it's too far' – suggests (Barney, 1963: 54). Futhermore, her most interesting collection of poetry is also her most duplicitous. *Poems & Poèmes: autres alliances* (1920) is a bilingual collection, published simultaneously in New York and Paris; the first twenty-six poems are in English, the last twenty-four in French, with the two halves (or 'tongues') of the text separated by a transparent sheet of tissue paper on which is printed (within an oval) 'A casement ope at night/To let the warm love in'. The collection symbolizes, in part, Barney's commitment to effecting a *rapprochement* between two literatures.[13] However, many of the poems also celebrate doubleness and disguise, the masquerade, the layering of identity. In 'Avertissement', an English poem with a French title, Barney writes: 'Leaving art to artists – we, love's lovers, / keep for outworn Beauty a disguise. / . . . So making everything seem otherwise: / Associations are our deities!' (Barney, 1920: 20). In another poem from the collection,

'Double Being', the poet describes 'A natural being, yet from nature freed, / Like a Shakespearian boy of fairy breed – / A sex perplexed into attractive seeming / – Both sex at best, the strangeness so redeeming! –' (Barney, 1920: 15).

Almost all the poems in the *Poems & Poèmes* collection are written in the first person – whether singular or plural – and most of them in the 'I-You' form of address that Ellen Moers has identified as a characteristic of women's love poetry. Thus the immediate sense of dissonance which is one effect of Romaine Brooks's portraits appears more coherently voiced in Barney's poems, in spite of the fact that the poems themselves describe and celebrate a fragmentary or doubled, but always *in*coherent identity. Certainly the strong dislocation the viewer feels when first encountering Brooks's portraits can be achieved in literature. In Radclyffe Hall's *The Well of Loneliness*, for example, the reader is jarred by references to Stephen Gordon as 'she', the masculine proper noun disrupting the female pronoun. However, the historical consequences of assuming a masculine voice have been quite different from those of assuming the visible indicators of masculinity. There is historical evidence to suggest that patriarchal order is obsessed with the *visual* symbols of masculine power.[14] In *Surpassing the Love of Men* Lillian Faderman points out that throughout history lesbians were persecuted (often burned or drowned) for their sexual activities *if* they also cross-dressed as men, whereas if they engaged in the same activities in female dress, they were usually only reprimanded in the courts. She notes that the cross-dressing lesbian created more confusion about gendered roles, claimed male social privileges, and demonstrated her transgression publicly and deliberately in a manner that made her reform and return to conventional heterosexuality seem impossible. In other words, cross-dressing took the 'private' realm of the sexual into the public' sphere (Faderman, 1981: 47–61).

Perhaps Brooks's most direct use of a strategy of visual dissonance can be found in her portrait of *Peter [A Young English Girl]* (1923–4) (Figure 3) where the title directs the viewer to look again and to look differently. The young English girl in this case is the artist Gluck (a rapidly rising star in the London arts world), who was to become well known for her cross-dressing in the extensive press coverage of her exhibitions from 1924 until the 1930s (see Souhami, 1988). In Brooks's portrait, Gluck's immaculate suit jacket, starched white collar, and elegant green waistcoat echo the aristocratic male fashions Brooks had flaunted in her own self-portrait. The figure of the 'mannish' lesbian, together with the reasons for her emergence at the turn of the century, has received useful critical attention from Esther Newton (1984), Sonja Ruehl (1982) and Katrina Rolley (1990). Newton argues that 'in the nineteenth century and before' women cross-dressers were primarily from the working class, and that 'Public, *partial* cross-dressing among bourgeois women was a late nineteenth-century development' (1984: 558). She attributes this shift to two related factors: one was the modernist identification with sexual freedom as a reaction against

Romaine Brooks, *Peter (A Young English Girl)* (1923–4). Oil on canvas. 91.9 × 62.3 cm. National Museum of American Art, Smithsonian Institution, gift of the artist.

Victorian values; the other was the publication in 1895 of Havelock Ellis's 'Sexual inversion in women'.

> How could the New Woman lay claim to her full sexuality? For bourgeois women, there was no developed female sexual discourse; there [were] only male discourses – pornographic, literary, and medical – about female sexuality. To become avowedly sexual, the New Woman had to enter the male world, either as a heterosexual on male terms (a flapper) or as – or with – a lesbian in male body drag (a butch). (Newton, 1984: 573).

Thus cross-dressing provided a visual code by which middle- and upper-class lesbians – released into sexuality from a nineteenth-century discourse of 'romantic friendship' – could recognize each other. However, it is important to realize that the public construction of an identifiably lesbian sexuality postdated that of male homosexuality by approximately three decades. As Jeffrey Weeks points out,

> Despite the ambiguities, it is clear that by the end of the nineteenth century a recognisably 'modern' male homosexual identity was beginning to emerge, but it would be another generation before female homosexuality reached a corresponding level of articulacy. The lesbian identity was much less clearly defined, and the lesbian subculture was minimal in comparison with the male, and even more overwhelmingly upper class or literary. (Weeks, 1981: 115)[15]

The prior existence of a recognizably homosexual culture – especially as it was articulated by such Decadent and Symbolist poets as Baudelaire and given further visibility in the 1895 trial of Oscar Wilde – gave artists like Barney and Brooks a convention from which to draw in their construction of a specifically lesbian cultural identity. In adopting the voice of the Wildean epigrammist, or in assuming the costume of the dandy, Barney and Brooks deliberately invoke the cultural markers of a marginal, deviant and illegal sexuality. Significantly, they did this at a time when lesbianism itself (at least in Britain) was increasingly being brought 'into the scope of the Criminal Law' (Weeks, 1981: 116).

Certainly, such lesbian cross-dressers as Radclyffe Hall, whose image was engrained in the popular imagination as the result of the 1928 obscenity trial of her novel, *The Well of Loneliness*, have been criticized for having internalized Havelock Ellis's categories of female inversion. However, Sonja Ruehl argues (borrowing from Foucault) that the very 'process of categorization makes resistance to ... power possible' (Ruehl, 1982: 17), and we would add that the flamboyant transvestism of Hall, Gluck, and Brooks was an effective and strategic 'counter-discourse' (see Terdiman, 1985). It is in the context of an evolving lesbian counter-discourse that the subversive nature of Brooks's self-portrait and her paintings of other lesbian women becomes apparent. Rather than being read as either literal transcriptions of her 'reality' (i.e., projections of her suffering and emotional angst) or else as pastiches of Whistler or other Decadent artists, her painting needs to be read as part of an ongoing attempt by lesbian women to publicly identify and verify their sexuality. Part of that process included culturally imag(in)ing themselves from a perspective that simultaneously embodied their differences in a form that could be socially recognized.

The question of recognized by whom is taken up by Katrina Rolley in her analysis of the sartorial strategies of Radclyffe Hall and Una Troubridge. As Rolley suggests, there were different levels of interpreting the male cross-dressing of upper-class lesbians. While informed viewers recognized the lesbian implications of such attire, 'for viewers who were unaware of their sexuality, especially those distanced by class, their appearance might be (mis)read as part of the aristocratic tradition of eccentricity, especially since Radclyffe Hall was also a writer' (Rolley, 1990: 55). That they conformed to upper-class practices such as dressing for dinner and spending large sums on fashionable clothes sometimes overshadowed the lesbian implications of their dress. Furthermore, as Rolley points out, the fact that 'masculine' styles, including short hair and tailored suits (albeit in less extreme forms), were in vogue during the 1920s, led some people to conclude that Radclyffe Hall was simply adopting a form of 'high-brow modernism'.[16]

It should be emphasized that Barney and Brooks asserted their privileges of class in order to display a so-called deviant sexuality. Although both radically challenged prevailing social and sexual expectations that were placed upon women, neither was interested in a similar critique of the class structure. Both tended to view themselves as exceptional individuals. In Brooks's case this is perhaps best typified by her increasing withdrawal from society as well as her passionate friendship with the Italian poet, Gabriele D'Annunzio whom she approvingly regarded as a sort of Nietzschean superman (Brooks, unpublished and undated ts: 255), while Barney's own élitism and conservative politics are sadly evidenced by her Second World War support of Mussolini's Fascism (Jay, 1988: 34). Given their socially conservative commitment to individualism, it is not surprising that Barney and Brooks took up the styles of Wilde and Whistler, both of whom posed as aristocratic dandies. Here it is important to acknowledge the contradictions that are raised when a radical critique of sexual orientation operates within a largely conservative view of the class hierarchy. Such political and aesthetic contradictions clearly resist easy classification as either conservative or radical.

The dilemma of appearances is familiar to feminists, lesbians and other marginalized groups: how to be positively identified as different when that difference is 'always already' structurally denigrated and undesirable. Here it is worth pursuing the dynamics of the categorization of dominance/deviance since they shed light on the ways in which the original and copy distinction has been applied to Barney and Brooks. It is also important to emphasize that while the *socially* 'dominant' sexuality against which Barney and Brooks were defining themselves was not heterosexual femininity but heterosexual masculinity, the *culturally* dominant sexuality – that of the avant-garde – was in many ways that of masculine homosexuality, or at least masculine 'homosociality' (Sedgewick, 1985: see also Koestenbaum, 1989).

In 'The dominant and the deviant: a violent dialectic', Jonathan Dollimore (also borrowing from Foucault) describes how deviant groups become politically resistant through a series of negotiated stages. For instance, in the case of homosexuality, the group 'begins to speak on its own behalf, to forge its own identity and culture, *often in the self-same categories by which it has been produced and marginalized*, and eventually challenges the very power structures responsible for its "creation"' (Dollimore, 1986: 180, emphasis in original). The resistance of any marginal group therefore necessarily moves through a number of stages during which different strategies are most effective. As Dollimore emphasizes, especially at the early stages,

> for the subordinate, at the level of cultural struggle . . [a] simple denunciation of dominant ideologies can be dangerous and counter-productive. Rather, they have instead, or also, to be negotiated. There are many strategies of negotiation; I am concerned here with two: the transformation of the dominant ideologies through (mis)appropriation, and their subversion through inversion. (1986: 181–2)

Radclyffe Hall's *The Well of Loneliness*, with its 'conservative' portrait of an 'authentic' yet 'abject' lesbianism, is Dollimore's example of a strategy of transformation through (mis)appropriation, while Rita Mae Brown's *Rubyfruit Jungle* (1973) enacts a 'subversion through inversion' of heterosexual norms. Dollimore suggests that 'the complex changes of the intervening forty-five years' (185) enabled Brown's critique. However, the case of Barney and Brooks upsets any easy narrative of progress, for their constructions of lesbianism depended less on 'images of authenticity taken from the established order' (185) than on the deliberate invocation and representation of *in*authenticity.[17]

In the case of Barney and Brooks, the second-hand need not be understood as second-rate but rather as a strategy of *recycling* images, voices, and costumes in the interest of creating a newly visible and deviant sexuality – albeit within the confines of an élitist and unproblematized social position. But to read Barney's and Brooks's work in its full complexity means calling into question our present rather narrow and discipline-bound notions of originality. Upsetting the signifying practices of the dominant social order entails not only finding new *forms* of writing and painting but the construction of new meanings, identities, and communities. In these terms, Brooks's *Self-Portrait* or *Peter [A Young English Girl]* are 'original' in the ways they (mis)appropriate the sartorial style of the decadent dandy for the socially élite lesbian. This exploration of the visual confusions of cross-dressing upsets an essentialist understanding of gender and overturns the notions of 'origin' and 'imitation' as they are used to regulate gendered identity. Evidently, Romaine Brooks was conscious of raising this problem in her painting when she noted in her autobiography that she was making great strides in her work and had 'already painted a series of solitary figures that had of life only the camouflage of exaggerated attire' (unpublished and undated ts: 210). Similarly, Barney's poem 'Love's Comrades' reads, in part, as a response to charges of poetic archaism and decadence:

> You say I've lived too long in France
> And wearied of the senses' dance?
>
> Like fresh air in an opium den
> You'll lead me out – to where? and when?
>
> . . . I fear no country's ready yet
> For our complexities . . . (Barney, 1920: 18)

In addressing the visual construction of gender in her painting is Brooks being any less avant-garde than, for example, the Cubist painters who were interested in the interrogation of single-point perspective? Is it that issues of perspective and science have been seen as more properly belonging to the realm of painting than sexuality and sartorial codes? Or is it that moving towards abstraction is still considered a purer, more complicated form of painting – that painting which addresses the problem of painting, or the medium's internal system of representation, is necessarily of a higher order than painting which addresses systems of visual representation outside the world of art? These questions are disturbing because it seems that we have not fully dismantled the negative stigma attached to representational art, especially when it deals with such ostensibly mundane and 'feminine' issues as fashion and sex-role stereotyping. Our inability to recognize such work as original rather than derivative perhaps reveals more about the limitations of our current critical apparatus than it does about Brooks's work. In an article addressing the implications of the intersection of feminist critiques of patriarchy and the postmodern critique of representation, Craig Owens has suggested that all too often the former has been subsumed by the latter (Owens, 1985). Has the possibility of writing the world differently through a form-breaking *écriture feminine* blinded us to the merits of alternative strategies that offer equally new ideas by reworking older forms? Ironically according to Owens, in our postmodern period,

> In the visual arts we have witnessed the gradual dissolution of once fundamental distinctions – original/copy, authentic/inauthentic, function/ornament. Each term now seems to contain its opposite, and this indeterminacy brings with it an impossibility of choice or, rather, the absolute equivalence and hence interchangeability of choices. Or so it is said. The existence of feminism with its insistence on difference forces us to reconsider. (Owens, 1985: 77).

The irony is that, while we can celebrate the dismantling of the original/copy distinction by today's visual and literary artists, we have been less sceptical about the way these terms have been deployed in relation to the work of earlier periods.

Notes

Bridget Elliott teaches in the Department of Art and Design and Jo-Ann Wallace in the Department of English at the University of Alberta, Canada. They are currently completing a book entitled *Modernist (Im)Positionings: Representations of and by Women in Culture, 1900–1939*, which will be published by Routledge. Research for this article was supported by a Social Sciences and Humanities Research Council of Canada grant.

An earlier version of this paper was first presented at the Twentieth-Century Literature Conference at the University of Louisville, 25 February 1989. Special thanks are extended to A. G. Purdy for advice on translation. Our thanks also to Alison Light of *Feminist Review* for her comments.

1 On the feminizing of the marginal, see Jardine (1985). The implications of Jardine's study of the 'woman effect' or how eminent male writers have introduced and used the term 'woman' in discourse (Jardine does not analyze the work of women writers) is discussed by Suleiman (1988). As Battersby (1990: 14) points out, the emphasis on originality is part of a long-standing conception of the artist as creator, or Godlike authority who imposes meaning and significance on formless matter.

2 Three important solo exhibitions of Romaine Brooks's work were mounted in 1925: first in Paris at the Galerie Jean Charpentier from 20 March – 3 April; then in London at the Alpine Club Gallery from 2–20 June; and lastly in New York City at the Wildenstein Galleries from 20 November – 31 December.

3 Greenberg's 1939 essay, 'Avant-garde and kitsch' set the terms of a continuing debate, heroizing the avant-garde by ascribing to it a 'superior consciousness of history' born out of 'the first bold development of scientific revolutionary thought in Europe' (Greenberg, 1961: 4). In 'search of the absolute' the avant-garde owes 'obedience' only to 'some worthy constraint or original'; that is, 'to the disciplines and process of art and literature themselves' (Greenberg, 1961: 5–6). It is, however, significant that Greenberg's construction of the avant-garde depends upon his construction of 'kitsch' as its binary opposite. Unlike Greenberg, Bürger's definition of the avant-garde is not dependent upon the construction of a binary opposite. The avant-garde is distinguished from other art movements not by its style but by its project, the targeting of 'art as an institution, and the course its development took in bourgeois society' (Bürger, 1984: 22). This includes an attack upon the category of individual production and individual reception of works of art, together with an attack upon the idea of the work of art as 'organic' and necessarily original. Bürger's *Theory of the Avant-Garde* obviously has much to offer a feminist analysis of the construction of the avant-garde; however, as with Krauss and Greenberg, his failure to consider the function of gender in the historical avant-garde is revealing, for his theory cannot account for the ways in which art functioned for a social group which maintained an always tangential and often ironic relation to bourgeois rationality.

4 These are the words used enthusiastically by Charles Eldrege, Director of the Smithsonian Museum, in Breeskin, 1986: 11. He fails to see any problem with having a legendary life.

5 In 1902 Natalie Barney inherited $2.5 million from her father, Albert Clifford Barney, himself heir to the Barney Car Works fortune; Romaine Brooks also came into her inheritance – her maternal grandfather had amassed a fortune from coal mines in Salt Lake City and Kingston, Pennsylvania – in 1902. Their money enabled them to live and work completely independently – unconstrained by any market considerations – in Paris, where Barney established her famous lesbian salon. For a further discussion of the cultural implications of their wealth, see Bridget Elliott and Jo-Ann Wallace, 'More than pin money: economies of representation in women's modernism' in *Im(ag)ining Women*, edited by Shirley Neuman and Glennis Stephenson (Northeastern UP, forthcoming).

6 Breeskin notes that portraits by Brooks were much sought after by members of fashionable society which gave her enormous leeway in her selection of subjects. She worked slowly, took on few commissions, and usually refused to sell her paintings.

7 Sutherland and Nochlin (1976: 268) discuss the accuracy of Brooks's autobiography. While certain aspects of Brooks's life may have been difficult, her emphatic depiction of herself as an outsider perpetuates the romantic mythology of the creative artistic genius, particularly in Decadent and early twentieth-century avant-garde circles. This is something that is overlooked by such critics as Secrest, 1974; Langer, 1981; and Gubar, 1981.

8 For instance, although Joshua Reynolds was interested in elevating the status of his portraits in late eighteenth-century England by introducing classical motifs into them, he still ranked the genre below history painting. This is discussed in his fourth discourse where he juxtaposes invention and copying. As far as the avant-garde is concerned, the status of portraiture seriously declined after the emergence of commercial portrait photography in the mid-nineteenth century. For further discussion of this issue, see Saisselin, 1963.

9 Barney was called 'l'Amazone' by Remy de Gourmont who first published his 'Lettres à l'Amazone' in the *Mercure de France* in 1913, and then published them in book form in 1914. Gourmont's élitist politics are evidenced in his 'Sur la hierarchie intellectuelle' *La Plume* 124 (15–30 June 1894): pp. 251–4, and had a profound influence on such American writers as Natalie Barney and Ezra Pound. See also Silverman (1989: 71).

10 Battersby futher notes that 'The originality of the art-work was not seen as a reflection of the external world, but of the mind and the personality that brought that work into existence. Consequently the artist's own character also became significant' (Battersby, 1990: 13).

11 'A Pilgrimage', from the *Poems & Poèmes: autres alliances* volume is one example. It reads, in part,

> Is that your window with the moving shade
> In pilgrimage I've come so far to see?
> – The air may enter, you are not afraid
> Of the 'great air' that plays invisible
> About your neck, moving your opened hair
> (That busy shadow is perhaps your maid?)
> While I must wait, as near as I may be . . . (Barney, 1920: 27)

12 'in fact, Romaine Brooks belongs to no time, to no country, to no circle, to no school, to no tradition; nor is she in revolt against these institutions; but rather, like Walt Whitman, neither for nor against them, she doesn't know what they are. She is the embodiment, the "flowering heights" of a civilization in decline, whose face she has managed to capture' [our translation].

13 In a 1926 letter to Gertrude Stein, Barney writes: 'The other night "au cameleon" I realized how little the french "femme de lettres" know of the english and Americans and vice versa . . . I wish I might bring about a better "entente" and hope therefore to organize here this winter, and this spring, readings and presentations that will enable our mind-allies to appreciate each other' [errors in original]. This letter traces the origins of the Academie de Femmes which Barney instituted in 1927. (Letter dated 16 December 1926, in the Beinecke Rare Book and Manuscript Library, Yale University.)

14 This was observed by Norman Bryson in his lecture on the work of Gericault delivered as part of the Henry Kreisel Lecture Series in 'Literature and the Visual Arts' held at the University of Alberta, January 1990.

15 Weeks goes on to argue that:

> It is striking that it is amongst the new professional women of the 1920s that the articulation of any sort of recognisable lesbian identity became possible for the first time, and it was indeed in the 1920s that lesbianism became in any way an issue of public concern, following a series of sensational scandals. (Weeks, 1981: 116)

16 Rolley draws this quote from a contemporary newspaper review of Radclyffe Hall's evening attire which appeared in the *Newcastle Daily Journal* 22 August 1928 (Rolley, 1990: 57).

17 Significantly, Dollimore's examples suggest (perhaps unintentionally) a continuing lesbian discourse of authenticity while he emphasizes a continuing homosexual discourse (through Oscar Wilde, Jean Genet, and Joe Orton) which is committed to 'the subversion of authenticity' (Dollimore, 1986: 189). Our analysis of the case of Barney and Brooks indicates that the latter was a strategy adopted by at least some lesbians some years before the publication of *The Well of Loneliness*.

References

BARNEY, Natalie Clifford (1920) *Poems & Poèmes: autres alliances* Paris: Emile-Paul Frères; New York: George H. Doran.

—— (1929) 'Romaine Brooks: Le cas d'un grand peintre du visage humain,' *Adventures de l'esprit* pp. 245–9, Paris: Emile-Paul Frères.

—— (1963) 'On writing and writers' trans. Ezra Pound, *Selected Writings* Miron Grindea, editor, London: Adam Books.

BATTERSBY, Christine (1990) *Gender and Genius: Towards a Feminist Aesthetics* Bloomington: Indiana University Press.

BENSTOCK, Shari (1986) *Women of the Left Bank: Paris, 1900–1940* Austin: University of Texas Press.

BREESKIN, Adelyn D. (1986) *Romaine Brooks* Washington: National Museum of American Art, Smithsonian Institute.

BROE, Mary Lynn and INGRAM, Angela (1989) editors, *Women's Writing in Exile* Chapel Hill: University of North Carolina Press.

BROOKS, Romaine (undated) *No Pleasant Memories* unpublished typescript. Short quotations by permission of the National Collection of Fine Arts Research Materials on Romaine Brooks, Archives of American Art, Smithsonian Institution.

BRUNT, Rosalind and ROWAN, Caroline (1982) editors, *Feminism, Culture and Politics* London: Lawrence & Wishart.

BULLEN, J. B. (1981) editor, *Vision and Design* London: Oxford University Press.

BÜRGER, Peter (1984) *Theory of the Avant-Garde* trans. Michael Shaw, Minneapolis: University of Minnesota Press.

CHALON, Jean (1979) *Portrait of a Seductress: The World of Natalie Barney* trans. Carol Barko, New York: Crown Publishers.

CHAMBERLAIN, Lori (1988) 'Gender and the metaphorics of translation' *Signs* Vol. 13, pp. 454–72.

COLUMBIA UNIVERSITY, DEPARTMENT OF ART HISTORY AND ARCHAEOLOGY (1976) *Modern Portraits: The Self and Others* intro. Kirk Varnadoe, New York: Wildenstein.

CONNOLLY, Cyril (n.d.) 'Adam and the Amazon', unidentified press clipping in a box of clippings of Romaine Brooks in the Beinecke Library, Yale University.

DOLLIMORE, Jonathan (1986) 'The dominant and the deviant: a violent dialectic' *Critical Quarterly* Vol. 28, pp. 179–92.

DURO, Paul (1986) 'Demoiselles à copier during the Second Empire' *Woman's Art Journal* Spring/Summer, pp. 1–7.

—— (1988) 'Copyists in the Louvre in the middle decades of the nineteenth century' *Gazette des Beaux-Arts* Vol. 111, pp. 249–54.

EAGLETON, Terry (1977) 'Translation and transformation' *Stand* Vol. 19, pp. 72–7.

FADERMAN, Lillian (1981) *Surpassing the Love of Men* New York: William Morrow.

FRY, Roger (1981, rpt. 1920) 'Art and life' in BULLEN (1981).

GODARD, Barbara (1989) 'Theorizing feminist discourse/translation' *Tessera* Spring, pp. 42–53.

GREENBERG, Clement (1961) 'Avant-garde and kitsch' *Art and Culture: Critical Essays* Boston: Beacon Press.

GRINDEA, Miron (1962) editor, 'The Amazon of letters: a world tribute to Natalie Clifford Barney' *Adam: International Review* Vol. 29, pp. 3–162.

GUBAR, Susan (1981) 'Blessings in disguise: cross-dressing as re-dressing for female modernists' *Massachusetts Review* Vol. 22, pp. 477–508.

JARDINE, Alice (1985) *Gynesis: Configurations of Women and Modernity* Ithaca: Cornell University Press.

JAY, Karla (1988) *The Amazon and the Page: Natalie Clifford Barney and Renee Vivien* Bloomington: Indiana University Press.

KOESTENBAUM, Wayne (1989) *Double Talk: The Erotics of Male Literary Collaboration* New York: Routledge.

KRAUSS, Rosalind E. (1981) 'The originality of the avant-garde' *The Originality of the Avant-Garde and Other Modernist Myths* Cambridge, Mass.: The MIT Press, pp. 151–70.

LANGER, Sandra (1981) 'Fashion, character and sexual politics in some Romaine Brooks lesbian portraits' *Art Criticism* Vol. 1, pp. 25–40.

MAUCLAIR, Camille (1899) 'La Femme devant les peintres modernes' *La Nouvelle Revue* 2d ser., I, pp. 190–213.

MOERS, Ellen (1977) *Literary Women: The Great Writers* New York: Anchor Books.

NEWTON, Esther (1984) 'The mythic mannish lesbian: Radclyffe Hall and the New Woman' *Signs* Vol. 9, pp. 557–75.

NOCHLIN, Linda (1973) 'The realist criminal and the abstract law' *Art in America* September/November, pp. 25–48.

OWENS, Craig (1985, rpt. 1983) 'The discourse of others: feminists and post-modernism' *Postmodern Culture* London: Pluto Press, pp. 57–77.

POUND, Ezra (1976) 'Letters to Natalie Barney' edited with commentary by Richard Sieburth, *Paideuma* Vol. 5, pp. 279–95.

ROLLEY, Katrina (1990) 'Cutting a dash: the dress of Radclyffe Hall and Una Troubridge' *Feminist Review* No. 35, pp. 54–66.

RUEHL, Sonja (1982) 'Inverts and experts: Radclyffe Hall and the lesbian identity' in BRUNT and ROWAN (1982), pp. 15–35.

SAISSELIN, Remy G. (1963) *Style, Truth and the Portrait* Cleveland: Cleveland Museum of Art.

SCHENCK, Celeste and BRODZKI, Bella (1988) editors, *Life/Lines: Theorizing Women's Autobiography* Ithaca: Cornell University Press.

SCHENCK, Celeste (1989) 'Exiled by genre: modernism, canonicity, and the politics of exclusion' in BROE and INGRAM (1989) pp. 225–50.

SECREST, Meryle (1974) *Between Me and Life: A Biography of Romaine Brooks* Garden City, NY: Doubleday & Company.

SEDGEWICK, Eve Kosofsky (1985) *Between Men: English Literature and Male Homosocial Desire* New York: Columbia University Press.

SILVERMAN, Debora (1989) *Art Nouveau in Fin-de-Siècle France* Berkeley: University of California Press.

SOUHAMI, Diana (1988) *Gluck: Her Biography* London: Pandora.

SPIVAK, Gayatri Chakravorty (1976) 'Translator's preface' in Jacques Derrida, *Of Grammatology* Baltimore: Johns Hopkins University Press.

STEINER, George (1975) *After Babel: Aspects of Language and Translation* London: Oxford University Press.

SULEIMAN, Susan Rubin (1988) 'A double margin: reflections on women writers and the avant-garde in France' *Yale French Studies* Vol. 75, pp. 148–71.

SUTHERLAND, Ann and NOCHLIN, Linda (1976) *Women Artists: 1550–1950* Los Angeles: Los Angeles County Museum.

TERDIMAN, Richard (1985) *Discourse/Counter Discourse: The Theory and Practice of Symbolic Resistance in Nineteenth Century France* Ithaca: Cornell University Press.

WEEKS, Jeffrey (1981) *Sex, Politics and Society* London: Longman.

Magical House

Debs Tyler-Bennett

Spellbound house,
where a woman waits,
long fingers gripping gloves.
Viewed from her window
the darkened garden
takes on witch shapes.
She wishes a mythic incantation,
to change her to a tree.
Then she'd wait
for her love to pass below,
and let
leaves like white gloves
fall to earth.

**In Celebration:
Djuna Barnes (1892–1982).
Renee Vivien (1877–1909).**

Note

Debs Tyler-Bennett was born in Sutton-in-Ashfield in 1963, and now lives in Loughborough. In 1986 she graduated as an MA from SUNY, Brockport and is now studying for a Ph.D. on the life and works of Djuna Barnes, at the University of Leicester. She has had works published in *Writing Women* and *Scarlet Women*.

FEMINISM AND MOTHERHOOD:
An American Reading

Ann Snitow

I've just emerged from a bout of reading, a wide eclectic sampling of
what this wave of US feminism has had to say about motherhood. My
conclusions are tentative, and there's another study that I've learned
arises directly out of this one – a study of how feminists have *mis*read
our own texts on this subject. My reading came as the end point of a year
and a half of infertility treatments and, although I see now how heavy
that experience lies on my own readings, perhaps my misreadings, I've
also come to see that *anyone* doing this work is likely to worry about
where to stand. I want to criticize the pervasive pronatalism that has so
shaped my recent experience – a pronatalism not only in the culture at
large but also inside feminism – but this desire inevitably raises the
question: who is allowed to criticize pronatalism, to question the desire
for children? The mothers might feel it disingenuous to take on this
task; they have their children after all. And the childless are bound to
feel that their critique is a species of sour grapes. Certainly, women like
me who have tried so hard to have babies late might well feel sheepish
and hypocritical about mounting a heavy critique of pronatalism. Will
the lesbian community speak up with unembarrassed enthusiasm for
the child-free life? Not now. Far more typical at the moment is the recent
book *Politics of the Heart: A Lesbian Parenting Anthology*. (Although I
find there Nancy D. Polikoff's question to the community: 'Who is
talking about the women who don't ever want to be mothers?' Her
answer: 'No one.') (Pollack and Vaughn, 1987) In one of the best
collections of essays about the decision to mother I've found, *Why
Children?*, the editors say they searched for mothers unhappy with
motherhood and they found them; but they could not get these mothers
to write (Dowrick and Grundberg, 1981). The dissatisfied mothers
feared hurting their children if they admitted how little they had liked
mothering. And what about the mothers who had children against their

will? Are they in a position to complain? Not really, once again: it will hurt the children to know they were unwanted. Besides, women have made an art of turning these defeats into triumphs; women have made a richer world out of their necessities. And so the children rarely hear a forthright critique of how women come to mother in a patriarchy – although, of course, they usually know all about it at one level or another, and guilt is left to fill in the holes of the story.

Women with children and women without them have been bristling at each other for years over the question of authenticity. The fight over the Equal Rights Amendment was a national example of this kind of warfare, but even inside feminism there's no particularly friendly entry point for this discussion. Which speaker has the necessary experience, hence the authority, to speak? Mothers can say they've seen both sides, can make judgements about what motherhood is like. Initiates, they are the ones who can measure the true dimensions of the choice. It's harder to imagine what the nonmothers can tell about their condition. One rises each morning to children – and often, of course, all through the night – but does one rise to the counter-condition – Ah, another day without children? The two conditions are not precisely parallel. And each one has its own narrative taboos.

What I want to argue is that feminism set out to break *both* taboos – those surrounding the experiences of the mothers and of the non-mothers, but for reasons I find both inside our movement and even more in the American society in which that movement unfolded, in the long run we were better able to attend to mothers' voices (or at least to *begin* on that project) than we were able to imagine a full and deeply meaningful life without motherhood, without children. Finally, in the defensive Reagan years, feminist ambivalence and guilt about blaming mothers, and our ambivalence about becoming mothers ourselves, toned down and tuned out a more elusive discussion of what choice might mean if there were really two imaginable lives for women – with and without children.

Building a supportive culture for both the mothers and the non-mothers in a crucial feminist task, but in the rising national babble of pronatalism in the 1980s, listening to the mothers was a project subtly susceptible to co-optation. Meanwhile, although I certainly felt that feminism was my shield at the infertility clinic, and that the often desperate women I met there were relatively lucky to be experiencing this loss of a baby now, when feminism is in the air, when middle-class married women work, when the birth rate is 1.9 children per woman, not the 3.7 of 1956, none the less feminist culture didn't seem to be producing alluring images or thinkable identities for the childless. What feminist idea about independence of work or political life seemed bracing enough to counter the yearning miasma of the infertility clinic? Could one turn to the feminist critique of the new reproductive technologies? Middle class and well informed, the women in infertility support groups (set up by the national organisation, *Resolve*) had already intimated most of the useful social and medical feminist analysis in books like Andrea Eagan's, Barbara Katz Rothman's, Gina Correa's and Barbara Stanworth's. Certainly, we all knew we were test animals (for example, record-keeping was the major undertaking at the clinic I attended), but this knowledge of the down-sides of medicalization had little bearing on the questions of our desire and need. Where was the feminist critique of our motivation? Why were we such eager consumers of twice-daily injections of pergonal, and mood-altering progesteron?

In 1970, feminism would have been quite hostile to these extreme undertakings, but that can't help anyone now. Indeed, it may well be that that earlier reaction to the pressure to mother was so historically specific that it can have no direct descendants. Young women now can be angry about the threat to abortion without feeling the terrible claustrophobia about the future my generation felt as children of the 1950s. All the same, historical shifts like these cannot fully explain the current flaccidity of the critique of motherhood in feminism. Surely we can't claim that young women have made peace with mothers, or that mothers now have social services or more help, so where has the rage gone? Why does the pronatalism of our period flourish with so little argument from us, the feminists?

To answer questions like these, I've begun to construct a time-line of feminism on motherhood. (This research is very much in progress and I hope readers will suggest titles, key moments, significant shifts as they also experienced them). Here are the main features of the line as it has emerged so far.

Although the record is complex, and although my generalizations are often contradicted by important exceptions, I see three distinct periods along the time-line. First, 1963 (Friedan, of course) to about 1974 – the period of what I call the 'demon texts', for which we have been apologizing ever since. Second, 1975 to 1979, the period in which feminism tried to take on the issue of motherhood seriously, to criticize the institution, explore the actual experience, theorize the social and psychological implications. In this period, feminists began on the project of breaking the first of the two taboos I mentioned earlier – the taboo on mothers' own descriptions of the fascination and joy of mothering (even in a patriarchy) and also the pain, isolation, boredom, murderousness.

By 1979, in a massive shift in the politics of the whole country, some feminist work shifts, too, from discussing motherhood to discussing families. Feminism continues to anatomize motherhood, but the movement is on the defensive. Certain once-desired changes recede as imaginable possibilities. In this period, feminists speak of 'different voices' and 'single mothers by choice'; the feminist hope of breaking the iron bond between mother and child seems gone, except in rhetorical flourishes, perhaps gone for good in this wave.

I'm going to try – briefly – to substantiate this periodization, but first a reminder: precision about generations is particularly important in a discussion of motherhood. In Paula Gidding's fine phrase, 'when and where I enter' matters. Each one has her own point of entry on this line.

None the less, the line has its own power to impose similar conditions, pressures, meanings on women of different ages, races, classes. The particular piece of feminist intellectual history I'm exploring here follows quite closely the trajectory of the baby-boom generation, what demographers call the mouse in the python, a large bulge travelling down the decades.

As Atina Grossmann has pointed out, this bulging generation is very powerful and continues to set its own rules. Its late child-bearing has made an upward blip on the generally descending graph of births per thousand. Its experiences disproportionately influence the social atmosphere. When it has babies, the stores are flooded with baby food. The culture this group creates, including the culture of feminism, shapes the era I'm describing here. For the young, the next bit of the line remains a mystery. Current debates about the real meaning of black teenage pregnancy and the low rate of marriage and fertility among college students give hints of how women may now be experimenting with the placement of children in their life cycles. It's a cheerful thought that many readers of this journal will have experiences that don't correspond to this outline.

Period 1: 1963 to about 1975

1963 is the year of *The Feminine Mystique*. The inadequacies of that book are well known. For example, in *From Margin to Center* (1984), bell hooks flips Friedan's story of the home-bound misery of the suburban housewife: for black women of the same period, paid work (which Friedan recommends for middle-class women) was usually drudgery, alienated work; work in the home seemed far more satisfying. Many have criticized Friedan's classism, racism, homophobia, her false universals. But Friedan herself has ignored all this and criticized *The Feminine Mystique* on different grounds altogether. In *The Second Stage* (1981), Friedan blames her earlier book for being antifamily, for trying to pry women away from children, and for overemphasizing women as autonomous individuals. In fact, *The Feminine Mystique* is rather mild on these points; it says nothing most feminists wouldn't agree to today about the need for women to have some stake in the world beyond their homes.

The Feminine Mystique is the first of my demon texts, by which I mean books demonized, apologized for, endlessly quoted out of context, to prove that the feminism of the early seventies was, in Friedan's words of recantation, 'strangely blind'. She excoriates her earlier self for thinking too much about 'women alone, or women against men', but not enough about 'the family'. In retrospect, it's an amazing thing that books in the early seventies dared to speak of 'women alone, or women against men'. It was, plain and simple, a breakthrough. Yet we've been apologizing for these books and often misreading them as demon texts ever since.

The most famous demon text is Shulamith Firestone's *The Dialectic of Sex: The Case for Feminist Revolution* (1970). This book is usually the starting point for discussions of how feminism has been 'strangely blind' about motherhood. Certainly, there are few of its sentences that Firestone would leave unmodified if she were writing with the same intent today. Her undertheorized enthusiasm for cybernetics, her self-hating disgust at the pregnant body ('Pregnancy is barbaric'), her picture of the female body as a prison from which a benign, nonpatriarchal science might release us have all dated. Her call for an end to childhood – although more interesting, I think, than scoffers have been prepared to grant – doesn't resonate with any experience of children at all. Finally, though, it's her tone we can't identify with, the sixties atmosphere of free-wheeling, shameless speculation. Part of the demonizing of this text arises out of a misreading of genre. *The Dialectic of Sex* is an example of utopian writing. (Some of this atmosphere has now been reclaimed – at least for academic feminism – in such work as Donna Haraway's (1985) 'Manifesto for Cyborgs'.)

Besides this tendency by feminists as well as nonfeminists to misread the tone and genre of *The Dialectic of Sex*, everyone colludes in calling it a mother-hating book. Search the pages; you won't find the evidence. I find instead:

> At the present time, for a woman to come out openly against motherhood on principle is physically dangerous. She can get away with it only if she adds that she is neurotic, abnormal, childhating and therefore 'unfit' . . . This is hardly a free atmosphere of inquiry. Until the taboo is lifted, until the decision not to have children or not to have them 'naturally' is at least as legitimate as traditional childbearing, women are as good as forced into their female roles. (Firestone, 1970: 199–200)

In other words, Firestone's work is reactive and rhetorical. The point is always 'smash patriarchy', not mothers.

Of course, there are real demon texts inside feminism, callow works like a few of the essays in the collection *Pronatalism: The Myth of Mom and Apple Pie* (Pek and Senderowitz, 1974), which reject childbearing in favour of having unsoiled white rugs and the extra cash to buy them. There's also some panic during this period about the new term then, the 'population explosion'. An ecology influenced by feminism has reinterpreted this material for us since, but some of the early essays talk as if once again it's up to women to populate the world properly, this time by abstaining from a killing *over*production of children.

But, inside feminism, such moments are rare. Instead I found extreme rhetoric meant to break the inexorable tie between mothers and children. For example, Lucia Valeska in 'If all else fails, I'm still a mother': 'All women who are able to plot their destinies with the relative mobility of the childfree should be encouraged to take on at least one existing child . . . to have our own biological children today is personally and politically irresponsible' (1975: 82–3). In the demonizing mode it's easy to hear this as a party line with biological mothers as self-indulgent backsliders. I hear in it, too, an effort to imagine a responsibility to kids which is not biological. The early texts are trying to pull away from the known and, like all utopian thinking, they can sound thin, absurd, undigested. But mother-hating? No.

The real demon texts I've found in my first period are works of social science outside feminism like the Moynihan report of 1965 on the so-called 'tangled pathology' of the black family. Mother really *is* named as the problem there, and the cure? More power for fathers! Black feminists often have to wrestle with this text when they set out to write about the motherhood experience. Ambivalence about the culture of black mothering is hard to express in the same universe where one has also to find ways to contradict the Moynihan report.

Finally, in my search for early feminist mother-hating what I found was – mostly – an absence. In the major anthologies like *Sisterhood is Powerful*, *Women in a Sexist Society* and *Liberation Now!* there are hardly any articles on any aspect of mothering. Nothing strange, really, about this blindness. The mouse had only just started down the python; most of the writers were young.

The exceptions, such as several articles in Leslie Tanner's *Voices from Women's Liberation* (1970), offer a programme that is unexceptionable even today – for example, Vicki Pollard's 'Producing society's babies' or the much reprinted 'On day care' by Louise Gross and Phyllis MacEwan. This second piece argues mildly that women shouldn't just want day care because it will liberate *them*, but also because day care is good for kids, too.

The revisions between the *Our Bodies/Ourselves* which was a newsprint booklet in 1971 and the glossy tome *Ourselves and Our Children* of 1978 reveals, I think, the hidden dynamics of our alienation from that earlier time. Under the section 'Pregnancy', the early version says such things as: 'We, as women, grow up in a society that subtly leads us to believe that we will find our ultimate fulfillment by living out our reproductive function and at the same time discourages us from trying to express ourselves in the world of work' (73). Only after pages and pages of reassurance that 'we as women can be whole human beings without having children' (74) does the 1971 text finally ask, 'What are the positive reasons for having children?' (76). The feminism of 1970 established a harsh self-questioning about a motherhood which formerly had been taken for granted.

But soon, very soon, this pre-emptory and radical questioning was misread as an attack on housewives. This has been as effective an instance of divide-and-conquer as I know. By the late seventies, both the mothers and the nonmothers were on the defensive. What a triumph of backlash, with internal dynamics which have been fully explored by Faye Ginsburg (1989) and others, feminists seeking to understand the special bitterness among women in our era.

The rewriting of the material on whether or not to have a child, in the *Ourselves and Our Children* of 1978, carries me into my second period, 1976 to 1980.

Period 2: 1976–1979

The 1978 text couldn't be more different from the earlier version of *Our Bodies/Ourselves*. It acknowledges that 'until quite recently' having a baby wasn't really considered a decision, but then goes on to assume that all that has changed, ending with this gee-whiz sentence: 'Now almost 5% of the population has declared its intentions to remain child-free' (17).

This is a liberal text, celebrating variety without much concern for uneven consequences. Both people who have decided to have children and people who have decided against are quoted at some length; but the effect is false symmetry, with no dialectic tension. The proliferation of people's reasons here is useful and instructive, an effort to get at difference, but the structural result is an aimless pluralism, a series of life-style questions, no politics.

But if in my description of *Ourselves and Our Children* I'm using the word liberal perjoratively, this my second period is also liberal in the best sense of the word: a time of freer speech, wider inquiry, a refusal of orthodoxy, an embrace of the practical reality. In these years the feminist work of exploring motherhood took off, and books central to feminist thinking in this wave were written, both about the daily experience of being a mother and about motherhood's most far-reaching implications.

1976 alone saw the publication of Adrienne Rich's *Of Woman Born*, Dorothy Dinnerstein's *The Mermaid and the Minotaur*, Jane Lazarre's *The Mother Knot*, and Linda Gordon's *Woman's Body, Woman's Right*. Also in that year, French feminism began to be a power in American feminist academic thinking. *Signs* published Hélène Cixous' 'The laugh of the Medusa' which included these immediately controversial words: 'There is always within [woman] at least a little of that good mother's milk. She writes in white ink'. Mysteries and provocations – which introduced a flood!

My Mother/Myself (1971), Nancy Friday's book, popularized the motherhood discussions in feminism, though it has often been criticized as essentially a daughter's book. Julia Kristeva split the page of *Tel Quel* down the middle in that year in 'Love's heretical ethics'; she was digging for the semiotic, the mother language of the body before speech. And 1978: Nancy Chodorow's *The Reproduction of Mothering* and Michelle Wallace's *Black Macho and the Myth of the Super-Woman*. These books were events. The intellectual work of feminism has its renaissance in these years. Not only does this period give rise to important work but also to fructifying debate.

Rachel DuPlessis introduced the brilliant special issue of *Feminist Studies* on motherhood in 1978 with an encomium to Rich's *Of Woman Born*. She honoured what Rich was trying to do – to pry mothering away from the patriarchal institution, *motherhood*. But then, DuPlessis went on to worry that Rich might be over-reacting, overprivileging the body. DuPlessis wrote, 'If, by the process of touching physicality, Rich wants to find that essence beyond conflict, the place where all women necessarily meet, the essence of woman, pure blood, I cannot follow there. Discussions like these inaugurate our continuing debates about essentialism, the body and social construction.

DuPlessis says she won't discuss practical politics, but she does ask the larger political question that nags throughout the period but is rarely addressed: which construction of motherhood is productive for feminist work? If we take Dinnerstein at her word, we're trying to get men to be mothers. If we follow Rich, our energies move towards building a female culture capable of the support not only of women but also of their children. Neither author would put these implications so baldly, without shading. Yet these texts create rival political auras and feminist theory is still far from sorting out the implications for activism of this great period of groundbreaking work.

It's important to add that, right in the middle of this period, in 1977, the first Hyde Amendment was passed; we lost Medicaid abortion. Abortion – the primal scene of this wave, won, to our amazement, in 1973, was only affordable for all classes for *four years* before this barely established right began slipping away again. While feminist thinkers were elaborating on the themes of motherhood, that other question – whether or not mothering is to remain a female universal – was slipping, slipping away. Feminist work of this period largely ignores the subject of my second taboo, the viability of the choice not to mother. Meanwhile the New Right was mounting a massive offensive against all efforts to separate women and mothering.

Period 3: 1980–1990

My second period ends – and my third begins – with the important threshold article by Sara Ruddick in 1980, 'Maternal thinking'. This piece pushed the work of the late seventies to some logical conclusions. Ruddick took seriously the question of what women actually *do* when they mother. She developed a rich description of what she called 'maternal practice' and 'maternal thinking'. A whole separate study deserves to be made of how this much-reprinted article has been read, reread, misread, appropriated into a variety of arguments. Ruddick herself says that the implications for feminism of her splendid anatomy of mothering are unclear. Is motherhood really a separable practice? Are its special features capable of translation into women's public power? Does motherhood have the universality Ruddick's work implies? Does the different voices argument (also developed by Carol Gilligan in 1982) lead to a vigorous feminist politics?

This is not even the beginning of a proper discussion of Ruddick but, for my purposes here, it's important to point out that Ruddick herself says that her book is not really about what feminism should say or do about mothering. Rather, it provides one of the best descriptions feminism has of *why* women are so deeply committed to the mothering experience, even under very oppressive conditions. Ruddick's work is a song to motherhood – multiphonic, without sugar – but still a song. 'Maternal thinking' is the fullest response since Adrienne Rich to the call to end my first taboo, the taboo on speaking the life of the mother.

It leaves my other taboo untouched, but this might well have seemed benign neglect in any other year but 1980. It was not part of Ruddick's intention to publish her work in the same year Reagan was elected, yet the meeting of the twain is, I think, part of this small history of feminism on motherhood.

Ruddick argues – with much reason – that hers is a specifically anti-Reagan text: it includes men as mothers; it includes lesbians as mothers; it demands public support for women's work. But it is extremely difficult to do an end-run around Reaganism by a mere proliferation of family forms. The left tried it; feminism tried it; everyone failed. (I'm thinking of Michael Lerner's Friends of Families organizing between about 1979 and 1982. I'm thinking of NOW's National Assembly on the Future of the Family in November of 1979. I'm thinking of Betty Friedan's retreat in *The Second Stage* of 1981). As Barbara Ehrenreich and others pointed out, the word 'family' was a grave in which the more autonomous word 'women' got buried. The problem with defining any cohabiting group as family and leaving it at that was the disappearance of any discussion of power within that group. Arlie Hochschild's *The Second Shift* (1989) reaffirms what we already intimate from experience: women, not families, continue to do almost all domestic work.

My time-line for the eighties is a record of frustration, retrenchment, defeat and sorrow. Out of the Baby M case in 1986–7 in which a so-called surrogate mother battled for and lost custody of the child she had carried but contracted away before birth, comes Phyllis Chesler's *Sacred Bond* (1988), the very title unthinkable a decade earlier. Certainly, things weren't going our way, and the studies to prove it poured out. In 1986 and 1987 we get Chesler on the injustice of child-custody laws, including feminist-initiated reforms, and Lenore Weitzman's frightening figures about what happens to women after no-fault divorce.

1986: my peak year for backlash at least partially internalized by feminism, gives us Sue Miller's novel *The Good Mother* and Sylvia Ann Hewlett's *A Lesser Life*. *A Lesser life* concerns itself with the horrendous struggles of working mothers, that is of most mothers now. Hewlett, once a self-defined feminist, is now against the ERA and sees nothing but liberal blarney in legal-equality models. In this particularly mean season, in which mothers do everything without social supports, Hewlett wants protection. She simply can't imagine social support for childrearing except as special programmes for women, whom she assumes will be the main ones responsible for children forevermore. Hewlett blames feminism for not making demands on the state. Of course we *did* make them. Our failure to win is a complex, historical event Hewlett oversimplifies. Further, one might argue that Hewlett's assumption, that women will inevitably do most of the childrearing, is broadly shared by the men in power, too, and that this attitude itself is one reason it is hard to coerce the state to do the work.

There are exceptions to backlash thinking on the eighties time-line, of course, although several turned out to be books and articles published elsewhere (I find my line doesn't work outside the US). Kathleen Gerson's *Hard Choices: How Women Decide About Work, Careers and Motherhood* (1985) tried to get at how profoundly women's lives are being changed by work. Sacred bond or not, women are simply spending less of their lives on mothering, more and more on a variety of other things. This book was among the very few I found that tried to address my second taboo, to take seriously the idea that women may well come to see mothering as one element in life, not its defining core. However raggedly, the women Gerson interviewed are already living out basically new story lines, making piecemeal changes over which feminism must struggle to preside.

Also during this period have come the great books on abortion: Rosalind Petchesky's *Abortion and Women's Choice* and Kristen Luker's *Abortion and the Politics of Motherhood* in 1984 and Faye Ginsburg's *Contested Lives* in 1989. But on the political front it's been some time since feminists demanding abortion have put front and centre the idea that one good use to which one might put this right is to choose not to have kids *at all*. Chastised in the Reagan years, pro-choice strategists – understandably – have emphasized the right to wait, the right to space one's children, the right to have each child wanted. They feared invoking any image that could be read as a female withdrawal from the role of nurturer.

Broad societal events like the steady rise of divorce and women's increasing workplace participation collide with women's failure to get day care, child support, fair enough custody laws, changes in the structure of a work day and a typical work life, and finally any reliable, ongoing support from men. Our discouragement is, in my view, the subtext of most of what we have written about motherhood in the past decade. I think women are heartbroken. Never has the baby been so delicious. We are – in this period of reaction – elaborating, extending, reinstitutionalizing this relation for ourselves. Mary Gordon writes in *The New York Times* book review (1985): 'It is impossible for me to believe that anything I write could have a fraction of the importance of the child growing inside me.' A feminist theorist tells me she is more proud of her new baby than of all her books.

I don't mean to criticize these deep sentiments but to situate them. They are freely expressed now; in 1970, feminist mothers, like all mothers, were briefly on the defensive, and ecstatic descriptions of mothering were themselves taboo. But now, since 1980, that brief past, with whatever its excesses or limitations, feels long gone. Even the still acceptable project of elaborating the culture of motherhood tends now to leave out the down part of the mother's story – her oppression, fury, regrets. One can't speak blithely of wanting an abortion anymore nor sceptically about the importance of motherhood. In the 1980s we have apologized again and again for ever having uttered what we now often name a callow, classist, immature or narcissistic word against mothering. Instead, we have praised the heroism of women raising children alone, or poor, usually both. We have embraced nurturance as an ethic, sometimes wishing that men would share this ethic without much hoping they will, and we have soldiered on, caring for the kids (in the US, more first children were born in 1988 than in any year on record), and continued to do 84 per cent of the housework. Complaints now have a way of sounding monstrous, even perhaps to our own ears. For here the children are, and if we're angry, in backlash times like these it's easy for feminism's opponents to insist that anger at oppression is really anger at children or at mothers. The New Right has been brilliant at encouraging this slippage, making women feel that being angry at the present state of mothering will poison the well of life. Guilt complicates feminist rage – and slows down feminist activism. There is the mother's guilt towards her children, and the nonmother's guilt that she has evaded this mass sisterhood now elaborated for us all as full of joy and pain, blood and passion, that she has evaded the central life dramas of intimacy and separation described so well in feminist writing about motherhood.

So, in conclusion, what? I hope it's clear that it's no part of my argument to say women shouldn't want children. This would be to trivialize the complexity of wishes, to call mothering a sort of false consciousness – a belittling suggestion. Women have incorporated a great deal into their mothering, but one question for feminism should surely be: Do we want this presently capacious identity, mother, to expand or to contract? How special do we want mothering to be? In other words, what does feminism gain by the privileging of motherhood? My reading makes more obvious than ever that feminists completely disagree on this point – or rather that there are many feminisms, different particularly on this point. And here's another viper's nest: do feminists want men to become mothers, too, that is, to have primary childcare responsibilities?

Again, the feminist work on this point veers wildly, is murky. Women disagree about what we should want – also about what we can get – from men. Bell hooks thinks we're afraid to let men know how really mad we are, afraid to finally confront them. That may be one reason we falter, but there are others: women ask, for example, 'Can men really nurture?' And behind that doubt, or that insult, hides our knowledge of what psychological power mothers have. Why give that up, we may well ask? I suspect that in addition, in our period, women are eager to establish that we don't really need men. This wave of feminism was a great outburst of indignation and it's important to us to feel that men are no longer necessary, particularly since lots of men are gone before the baby is two. In so far as patriarchy means the protective law of the father, patriarchy's over.

I find a great cynicism among us about ever getting men's help, or the state's. Because we have won so few tangible victories, women tend to adopt a sort of Mother Courage stance now – long suffering, almost sometimes a parody of being tireless.

But it occurs to me that, finally, this picture I'm painting is much too bleak. One can ask other questions that hint at a more volatile situation altogether. The low spirits of recent movement history are an irony. Actually, we are living in a moment in which women's identities are extremely labile and expanding. How do we feminists greet and interpret the fact that women are voting with their feet, marrying later, using contraception and abortion and having fewer children? Do we look forward to some golden age when parental leave, childcare and flexitime will have helped women so much that the birth-rate will rise again? Such a thought seems buried in the current feminist piety about abortion, that we want not only the right to abort but also the right to have children, etc. A worthy thought, but one that has not yet been fully examined. Are we to consider the lowered birth-rate merely one more proof that women are so over-worked they're ready to drop, or might there be some opportunities for feminism buried in these broad demographic changes?

Under what banner are we going to fly our demands for mothers? I like best the gender-neutral constructions of this cohort of the brilliant feminist lawyers. Yet, as they would be first to point out, gender-neutral demands – for parenting leaves, disability, gender-blind custody, have their short-term price. We give up something, a special privilege wound up in the culture-laden word 'mother' which we will not instantly regain in the form of freedom and power. We're talking about a slow process of change when we talk about motherhood; we're talking about social divisions which are still fundamental. Giving up the exclusivity of motherhood is bound to feel to many like loss. Deirdre English called this 'the fear that feminism will free men first'. Men will have the power of the world *and* the nurturant experience, the centrality to their children. Only a fool gives up something present for something intangible and speculative, Jack and the Beanstalk exchanging the cow for a couple of beans. But even if we can't yet imagine our passage from here to there, from control over motherhood to shared, socialized parenthood, couldn't we talk about it, structure demands? An epigram keeps forming in my mind: 'Just because you can't have something doesn't mean you don't want it or shouldn't fight for it.'

Let me end with a cautionary analogy: In the nineteenth century, feminism's *idée fixe* was the vote. We won it, but it was hard to make it mean something larger than mere voting, to make it into a source of public authority for women. In our wave, the *idée fixe* has been abortion. If we're lucky, and if we work very hard, we may win it. But just like with the vote, there will be much resistance to letting the right to abortion expand to its larger potential meaning. We seem – this time around – to really want abortion. And this right carries within it the seed of new identities for women.

Postscript

On 30 April 1991, I made a visit, kindly arranged by Hester Eisenstein, to the State University of New York at Buffalo, where a wonderful group addressed the question of the time-line.

The younger women in the room reported that they were under acute pressure to have children – and soon. We older ones felt consternation: what form does the pressure take? 'Medical. The media, doctors, other women all tell us that if we don't have children, we're opening ourselves to all kinds of diseases like endometriosis and uterine cancer.'

Dispirited about the current atmosphere, we compared this threat with the nineteenth century idea that if women went to college, their uteruses would shrivel up as their brains developed. At the same time, we noted for the record the problem with the counter-claim sometimes made by feminism that all medical limits set in a patriarchy are merely corrupt, that without patriarchy we could control our bodies. This misleading promise led some to assume late babies were no problem at all, and contributed to the very atmosphere which has brought so many women to put faith in erratic and experimental technologies which promise this elusive control.

In yet another turn of the argument, we worried that some recent feminist critiques of birth technology ignore advances on which we've come usefully to rely. Claire Kahane went so far as to wonder if some sectors of the ecology movement, by romanticizing 'the natural', had added to the pressures the younger women in the room were feeling to do 'the natural' thing.

We moved on to men: are men trying to break in upon the mother–child dyad with the new birth technologies, or with law suits against women who smoke, drink or take crack while pregnant? If the mother is the enemy of the foetus, the state becomes the paternal rescuer. These thoughts led us to question just how paranoid we wanted to be: male appropriations are legion and female scepticism is justly epidemic, but how, then, to leave the path open for men to make a more progressive move towards joining women and children?

Certainly, men still fade out of most motherhood discussions. For example, several reported that their college alumni magazines were flooded in the mid-1980s with reports from career women who didn't want to go to work anymore, who wanted to stay home with their kids. This was the new 'choice' of the middle class. What made this potentially rich option for variety and change ominous besides its unrepentent class-bound character was the utter lack of this 'choice' for men. The 'Mommy track' as it was called in the US was a revised work trajectory which would include time for children. Revolutionary if it were a rethinking of work for everyone, this corporate plan became a symbol of the continuing divide between male and female life-stories – with motherhood the signpost at the crossroads.

Thank you to the feminists of Buffalo.

In other responses, several women have questioned my observation that the US time-line of feminism on motherhood won't work for other countries. Marti Scheel writes that in the case she knows, West Germany, the line works if one starts three to five years later, as the baby boom was delayed there. Of course, I'd like to know what other readers outside the US think.

Greetings from New York.

Notes

Ann Snitow has been a feminist activist since 1970 when she was a founding member of New York Radical Feminists. She teaches literature and women's studies at Eugene Lang College of the New School for Social Research. With Christine Stansell and Sharon Thompson she edited *Desire: The Politics of Sexuality* (Virago) and she is currently writing *A Gender Diary*, a personal and theoretical account of the women's movement.

Time-Line: Feminism on Motherhood

Compiled by Ann Snitow and Carolyn Morell
Key: All items are feminist or feminist-related unless marked*. Items marked* are relevant articles and events.

1963
FREIDAN, Betty *The Feminine Mystique* New York: W. W. Norton & Co.

1964
ROSSI, Alice 'Transition to parenthood' *Journal of Marriage and the Family* Vol. 1, No. 30.

1965
*MOYNIHAN, Daniel Patrick 'The Negro Family: The Case for National Action'.

1969
WILLIS, Ellen 'Whatever happened to women? Nothing, that's the trouble' *Mademoiselle* September.
POLLARD, Vicki 'Producing society's babies' *Women: A Journal of Liberation* Fall.

1970
FIRESTONE, Shulamith *The Dialectic of Sex* New York: William Morrow.
TANNER, Leslie editor, *Voices From Women's Liberation* New York: Signet.

1971
BOSTON WOMEN'S HEALTH COURSE COLLECTIVE *Our Bodies, Ourselves* Boston: New England Free Press.
PECK, Ellen *The Baby Trap* New York: Pinnacle Books.
*COMPREHENSIVE CHILD DEVELOPMENT ACT passed by Congress, vetoed by Richard Nixon (Child care funds).

1973

RADL, Shirley *Mother's Day is Over* New York: Charterhouse.

GILDER, George *Sexual Suicide* New York: Quadrangle Books.

ROE v. WADE. The Supreme Court guarantees the abortion right.

1974

PECK, Ellen and SENDEROWITZ, Judith *Pronatalism: The Myth of Mom and Apple Pie* New York: Thomas Y. Crowell.

BERNERD, Jessie *The Future of Motherhood* New York: The Dial Press.

MITCHELL, Juliet *Psychoanalysis and Feminism: Freud, Reich, Laing, and Women* New York: Pantheon Books.

1975

HAMMER, Signe *Daughters and Mothers, Mothers and Daughters* New York: Quadrangle Books.

VALESKA, Lucia 'If all else fails, I'm still a mother' *Quest*, Vol. 1, No. 3, Winter.

1976

CHODOROW, Nancy and CANTRATTO, Susan 'The fantasy of the perfect mother' *Social Problems*, Vol. 23, No. 2.

CIXOUS, Hélène 'The laugh of the Medusa' *Signs* Vol. 1, No. 4, Summer: 875–93.

DINNERSTEIN, Dorothy *The Mermaid and the Minotaur: Sexual Arrangements and Human Malaise* New York: Harper & Row.

GORDON, Linda *Woman's Body, Woman's Right: Birth Control in America* Grossman Publishers.

LAZARRE, Jane *The Mother Knot* New York: McGraw-Hill.

RICH, Adrienne *Of Woman Born: Motherhood as Experience and Institution* New York: W. W. Norton.

RUSSO, N. F. 'The motherhood mandate' *Journal of Social Issues*, Vol. 32, No. 3.

1977

FRIDAY, Nancy *My Mother/Myself: The Daughter's Search for Identity* New York: Delacorte Press.

KLEPFISZ, Irena 'Women without children/women without families/women alone' reprinted in *Dreams of an Insomniac: Jewish Feminist Essays Speeches, and Diatribes* Eight Mountain Press (1990).

JOFFE, Carole *Friendly Intruders: Childcare Professionals and Family Life* Berkeley: University of California Press.

KRISTEVA, Julia 'Love's heretical ethics' *Tel Quel* 74, Winter: 39–49.

ROSSI, Alice 'A biosocial perspective on parenting' *Daedelus*, Vol. 106, No. 3.

*HYDE AMENDMENT No Medicaid abortions, end of abortions for poor women.

*LASCH, Christopher *Haven in a Heartless World* New York: Basic Books.

1978

CHODOROW, Nancy *The Reproduction of Mothering: Psychoanalysis and The Sociology of Gender* Berkeley: University of California Press.

BOSTON WOMEN'S HEALTH BOOK COLLECTIVE *Ourselves and Our Children: A Book by and for Parents* New York: Random House.

FEMINIST STUDIES Special Issue 'Toward a Feminist Theory of Motherhood' Vol. 4, No. 2, June.

HOFFNER, Elaine *Mothering: The Emotional Experience of Motherhood after Freud and Feminism* New York: Doubleday Inc.

WALLACE, Michele *Black Macho and the Myth of the Super-Woman* New York: The Dial Press.

1979

ARCANA, Judith *Our Mother's Daughters* Berkeley: Shameless Hussy Press.
CARASA (Committee for Abortion Rights and Against Sterilization Abuse) *Women Under Attack: Abortion, Sterilization Abuse and Reproductive Freedom* New York.
CHESLER, Phyllis *With Child: A Diary of Motherhood* New York: Thomas Y. Crowell.
FEMINIST STUDIES Special Issue 'Workers, Reproductive Hazards and the Politics of Protection' No. 5, Summer.
FRIEDAN, Betty 'Feminism takes a new turn' *The New York Times*, 26 August.
LORDE, Audre 'Man Child: a black lesbian feminist's response' *Conditions* 4.
WILLIS, Ellen 'The family: love it or leave it' *The Village Voice* v.XXIV, No. 38, 17 September: 1, 29–35.
LERNER, Michael 'Friends of Families' organizing drive, California, c. 1979–82.
NOW 'National Assembly on the Future of the Family' Conference, New York Hilton Hotel, 19 November.
'THE SCHOLAR AND THE FEMINIST VI: THE FUTURE OF DIFFERENCE' Conference, Barnard College, New York 29 April.

1980

BADINTER, Elizabeth *Mother Love: Myth and Reality* New York: Macmillan.
EHRENSAFT, Diane 'When men and women mother' *Socialist Review* 49, Vol. 10, No. 4, Summer.
EISENSTEIN, Hester and **JARDINE, Alice** editors, *The Future of Difference* Boston: G. K. Hall & Co.
MARKS, Elaine and **De COURTIVRON, Isabelle**, editors, *New French Feminisms, An Anthology* Amherst: University of Massachusetts Press.
OAKLEY, Ann *Becoming a Mother* New York: Schocken Books.
Women Confused: Toward a Sociology of Childbirth New York: Schocken Books.
RUDDICK, S 'Maternal thinking' *Feminist Studies* Vol. 6, No. 2, Summer: 342–67.
WEISSKOPF, Susan Contratto 'Maternal sexuality and asexual motherhood' *Signs* Vol. 5, No. 4, Summer.

1981

BRIDENTHAL, Renate, KELLY, Joan, SWERDLOW, Amy and **VINE, Phyllis**, editors, *Household and Kin: Families in Flux* New York: The Feminist Press.
BROWN, Carol 'Mothers, fathers, and children: from private to public patriarchy' reprinted in *Women and Revolution*, edited by Lydia Sargent, Boston: South End Press.
DOWRICK, Stephanie and **GRUNDBERG, Sibyl** *Why Children?* New York: Harcourt Brace Jovanovich.
FRIEDAN, Betty *The Second Stage* New York: Simon & Schuster.
HIRSCH, M. 'Mothers and daughters: a review' *Signs* Vol. 7, No.1.
LORBER, J., COSER, R. L., ROSSI, A. S. and **CHODOROW, N.** 'On *The Reproduction of Mothering*: a methodological debate' *Signs* Vol. 7, No. 1.
O'BRIEN, Mary *The Politics of Reproduction* New York: Routledge.
THE FAMILY PROTECTION ACT proposed.

1982

BARRETT, Michele and MCINTOSH, Mary *The Anti-Social Family* London: Verso.

GILBERT, Lucy and WEBSTER, Paula *Bound by Love: The Sweet Trap of Daughterhood* Boston: Beacon Press.

GILLIGAN, Carol *In a Different Voice: Psychological Theory and Women's Development* Cambridge and London: Harvard University Press.

LERNER, L. 'Reproduction of mothering: an appraisal' *The Psychoanalytic Review* Vol. 51, No. 1.

ROTHMAN, Barbara Katz *In Labor: Women and Power in the Birth Place* New York: W. W. Norton.

THORNE, Barrie and YALOM, Marilyn *Rethinking the Family: Some Feminist Questions* New York and London: Longman.

*ERA defeated.

1983

DALLY, Ann *Inventing Motherhood: The Consequences of an Ideal* New York: Shocken Books.

DANIELS, Pamela and WEINGARTEN, Kathy *Sooner or Later* New York: W. W. Norton.

DIAMOND, Irene editor, *Families, Politics and Public Policy: A Feminist Dialogue On the State* New York: Longman.

FOLBRE, Nancy 'Of patriarchy born: the political economy of fertility decisions' *Feminist Studies* Vol.9, No. 2, Summer.

PORTER, Nancy reviewing 'Mothering: essays in feminist theory' *Women's Studies Quarterly* Vol. VII, Winter.

RILEY, Denise *War in the Nursery: Theories of the Child and the Mother* London: Virago.

1984

ALPERT, J. L., GERSON, M. and RICHARDSON, M. S. 'Mothering: the view from psychological research' *Signs* Vol. 9, No. 3.

ARDITTI, Rita, KLEIN, Renate Duelli and MINDEN, Shelley *Test-Tube Women: What Future for Motherhood?* London and Boston: Pandora Press.

BOSTON WOMEN'S HEALTH BOOK COLLECTIVE *The New Our Bodies, Ourselves: A Book by and for Women* New York: Touchstone/Simon & Schuster.

DELPHY, Christine *Close to Home: A Materialist Analysis of Women's Oppression* Amherst: University of Massachusetts.

GERSON, Mary-Joan 'Feminism and the wish for a child' *Sex Roles*, Vol. VII September.

GIDDINGS, Paula *When and Where I Enter: The Impact of Black Women on Race and Sex in America* New York: William Morrow.

GREER, Germaine *Sex and Destiny: The Politics of Human Fertility* New York: Harper & Row.

HOOKS, Bell 'Revolutionary parenting' reprinted in *From Margin to Center* Boston: South End Press.

LUKER, Kristen *Abortion and the Politics of Motherhood* Berkeley and London: University of California Press.

PETCHESKY, Rosalind *Abortion and Women's Choice: The State, Sexuality, and Reproductive Freedom* New York: Longman.

RAPP, Rayna 'The ethics of choice: after my amniocentesis, Mike and I faced the toughest decision of our lives' *Ms*. April.

SEVENHUIJSEN, Selma and DEVRIES, Petra 'The women's movement and motherhood' reprinted in *A Creative Tension: Key Issues of Socialist Feminism: An*

International Perspective from Activist Dutch Women, 9–25 Boston: South End Press.

SIMONS, Margaret A 'Motherhood, feminism, and identity' *Women's Studies International Forum* Vol. 7, No. 5: 349–59.

TREBILCOT, Joyce editor, *Mothering: Essays in Feminist Theory* Totowa: Rowman & Allanheld.

1985

COREA, Gena *The Mother Machine: Reproductive Technologies from Artificial Insemination to Artificial Wombs* New York: Harper & Row.

FOLBRE, Nancy 'The pauperization of motherhood: patriarchy and public policy in the United States' *Review of Radical Political Economics*, Vol. 16, No. 4, Winter.

GERSON, Kathleen *Hard Choices: How Women Decide about Work, Career, and Motherhood* Berkeley and London: University of California Press.

GITTINS, Diana *The Family in Question* London and New York: Macmillan.

HARAWAY, Donna 'A manifesto for cyborgs: science technology, and socialist feminism in the 1980s' *Socialist Review* 80.

PIES, Cheri *Considering Parenthood* San Francisco: Spinsters Book Co.

RENVOIZE, Jean *Going Solo: Single Mothers by Choice* Boston: Routledge & Kegan Paul.

SCHULENBERG, Joy *Gay Parenting: A Complete Guide for Gay Men and Lesbians with Children.* New York: Anchor Press/Doubleday.

WEITZMAN, Lenore J *The Divorce Revolution: The Unexpected Social and Economic Consequences for Women and Children in America* New York: Free Press.

ZELIZER, Viviana *Pricing the Priceless Child: The Changing Social Value of Children* New York: Basic Books.

1986

ALLEN, Jeffner 'Motherhood: the annihilation of women' In *Lesbian Philosophy: Explorations* Palo Alto: Institute of Lesbian Studies.

ATWOOD, Margaret *The Handmaid's Tale* Boston: Houghton Mifflin Co.

BARRETT, Michele and HAMILTON, Roberta *The Politics of Diversity: Feminism, Marxism, and Nationalism* London: Verso.

CHESLER, Phyllis *Mothers on Trial: The Battle for Children and Custody* Seattle: Seal Press.

GERSON, Kathleen 'Emerging social divisions among women: implications for welfare state politics' *Politics and Society*, Vol. 15, No. 2: 213–24.

HERON, Liz 'Motherhood . . . to have or have not? In *Changes of Heart: Reflections on Women's Independence*, pp. 177–218, Boston: Pandora Press.

HEWLETT, Sylvia Ann *A Lesser Life: The Myth of Women's Liberation in America* New York: William Morrow.

HYPATIA Special Issue 'Motherhood and sexuality' Vol. 1, No. 2, Fall.

KANTROWITZ, Barbara 'Three's a crowd' *Newsweek* 1 September: 68–76.

MAIRS, Nancy 'On being raised by a daughter' *Plaintext* University of Arizona.

MILLER, Sue *The Good Mother* New York: Harper & Row.

MS Special Issue 'When to have your baby' December.

OMOLADE, Barbara 'It's a family affair: the real lives of black single mothers' *Village Voice*, 16 July.

ROTHMAN, Barbara Katz *The Tentative Pregnancy: Prenatal Diagnosis and the Future of Motherhood* New York: Viking.

*MCBROOM, Patricia A. *The Third Sex: The New Professional Woman* New York: William Morrow.

*NEW YORK TIMES MAGAZINE 'The American Wife' 26 October.

1987

EHRENSAFT, Diane *Parenting Together* New York: Free Press.

GENEVIE, Louis E. and **MARGOLIES, Eva** *The Motherhood Report: How Women Feel About Being Mothers* New York: Macmillan.

GLEVE, Katherine 'Rethinking feminist attitudes towards motherhood' *Feminist Review* 25, Spring.

MARTIN, Emily *The Woman in the Body: A Cultural Analysis of Reproduction* Boston: Beacon Press.

PETCHESKY, Rosalind 'Fetal images' *Feminist Studies*, Vol. 13, No. 2.

POLLACK, Sandra and **VAUGHAN, Jeanne** editors, *Politics of the Heart: A Lesbian Parenting Anthology* Ithaca: Firebrand Books.

PRUETT, Kyle *The Nurturing Father: Journeys Toward the Complete Man* New York: Warner Books.

ROSENFELT, Deborah and **STACEY, Judith** 'Second thoughts on the second wave' *Feminist Studies* Vol. 13, No. 2.

SEGAL, Lynne *Is the Future Female? Troubled Thoughts on Contemporary Feminism* New York: Peter Bedrick Books.

SEGAL, Lynne 'Back to the nursery' *New Statesman* 1 February.

SOJOURNER Special Issue 'Motherhood is political: the ideal vs the real'.

SPALLONE, Patricia and **STEINBERG, Lynn** *Made to Order: The Myth of Reproductive and Genetic Progress* New York: Pergamon Press.

STANWORTH, Michelle editor, *Reproductive Technologies: Gender, Motherhood and Medicine* Minneapolis: University of Minnesota Press.

*****TIME MAGAZINE** 'Here come the dinks' 20 April: 75.

*****WATTENBERG, Ben J.** 'The birth dearth' Pharos Books.

*****THE BABY M CASE** in the news.

1988

AGUERO, Kathi and **GORDETT, Marea** 'Mothering and writing: a conversation' *Women's Review of Books* July.

BENJAMIN, Jessica *The Bonds of Love: Psychoanalysis, Feminism, and the Problem of Domination* New York: Pantheon Books.

CARASA (Committee for Abortion Rights and Against Sterilization Abuse) *Women Under Attack: Victories, Backlash, and the Fight for Reproductive Freedom* edited by Susan E. Davis, Boston: South End Press, Pamphlet No. 7 (The Athene Series).

CHESLER, Phyllis *Sacred Bond: The Legacy of Baby M* New York: Times Books.

EISENSTEIN, Zillah R. *The Female Body and the Law* Berkeley and London: University of California Press.

EPSTEIN, Cynthia Fuchs *Deceptive Distinctions: Sex, Gender, and the Social Order* Boston: Yale University Press.

GRABUCHER, Marianne *There's a Good Girl: Gender Stereotyping in the First Three Years of Life: A Diary* trans. from the German by Wendy Philipson, London: The Women's Press Ltd.

HERMAN, Ellen 'Desperately seeking motherhood' *Zeta* March.

QUINDLEN, Anna 'Mother's choice' *Ms* February.

WEIDEGER, Paula 'Womb worship' *Ms* February.

WEINBERG, Joanna 'Shared Dreams: a left perspective on disability rights and reproductive rights' in *Women with Disabilities*, edited by Adrienne Asch and Michelle Fine. Temple.

*****FAMILY SUPPORT ACT** (*Workfare*).

1989

DOUGLAS, Susan J 'Otherhood' *In These Times* September: 12–13.

EDWARDS, Harriet *How Could You? Mothers Without Custody of Their Children* The Crossing Press.

FERGUSON, Ann *Blood at the Root: Motherhood, Sexuality, and Male Dominance* London: Pandora Press.

GERSON, Deborah 'Infertility and the Construction of Desperation' *Socialist Review* Vol. 19, No. 3, July/September.

GINSBURG, Faye D *Contested Lives: The Abortion Debate in an American Community* Berkeley and London: University of California Press.

HIRSCH, Marianne *The Mother-Daughter Plot: Narrative, Psychoanalysis, and Feminism* Indiana University Press.

HYPATIA Special Issue 'Ethics and reproduction' Vol. 4, No. 3, Fall.

HOCHSCHILD, Arlie *The Second Shift* London and New York: Viking Penguin.

OLIVIER, Christiane *Jocasta's Children: The Imprint of the Mother* New York: Routledge.

ROTHMAN, Barbara Katz *Recreating Motherhood: Ideology and Technology in a Patriarchal Society* New York: W. W. Norton.

RUDDICK, Sally *Maternal Thinking: Towards a Politics of Peace* Boston: Beacon.

SEVENHUIJSEN, S. and SMART, Carol editors, *Child Custody and the Politics of Gender* New York: Routledge.

1990

ARNUP, Katherine, LEVESQUE, Andree and PIERSON, Ruth Roach *Delivering Motherhood: Maternal Ideologies and Practices in the 19th and 20th Centuries* New York: Routledge.

CHAMBERLAYNE, Prue 'The mother's manifesto and disputes over "Mutterlichkeit"' *Feminist Review* No. 35, Summer: 9–23.

COLE, Ellen and KNOWLES, Jane Price editors *Woman-Defined Motherhood* Binghamton: Harrington Park Press.

EHRENSAFT, Diane 'Feminists fight (for) fathers' *Socialist Review* 4: 57–80.

FINGER, Anne *Past Due: A Story of Disability, Pregnancy, and Birth* Seattle: Seal Press.

GORDON, Tuula *Feminist Mothers* New York: New York University Press.

KAMINER, Wendy *A Fearful Freedom: Women's Flight from Equality* Addison-Wesley.

MORELL, Carolyn MacKelcan 'Unwomanly conduct: the challenges of intentional childlessness' Dissertation, Bryn Mawr.

O'BARR, Jean, et al., editors *Ties that Bind: Essays on Mothering and Patriarchy* Chicago and London: University of Chicago Press.

RAPPING, Elayne 'The future of motherhood: some unfashionably visionary thoughts' In *Women, Class, and the Feminist Imagination* edited by Karen V. Hanson and Ilene J. Philipson. Temple.

SANDELOWSKI, Margarete. 'Fault lines: infertility and imperiled sisterhood' *Feminist Studies*, Vol. 16, No. 1, Spring: 33–51.

WHITE, Evelyn C. editor, *The Black Women's Health Book: Speaking for Ourselves* Seattle: Seal Press.

WILT, Judith *Abortion, Choice, and Contemporary Fiction: The Armageddon of the Maternal Instinct* Chicago and London: University of Chicago Press.

QUALITATIVE RESEARCH, APPROPRIATION OF THE 'OTHER' AND EMPOWERMENT

Anne Opie

Introduction

The issues I want to explore in this essay have arisen in the context of my qualitative research into the everyday experiences of twenty-eight family caregivers caring for elderly confused spouses or relatives at home.[1] My interpretation of the interview data, derived from lengthy and unstructured interviews, has drawn extensively on feminist comment and research on caring in order to challenge conventional political and social knowledge about caring. Yet, in constructing an analysis which adequately represents the complexity of the experiences in which the interview texts are grounded, I have also become conscious of limitations in feminist interpretations. Although at one point they are liberatory because they open to inspection what has been previously hidden, they are also restrictive in the sense that they can appropriate the data to the researcher's interests, so that other significant experiential elements which challenge or partially disrupt that interpretation may also be silenced.

The significance of feminist analyses of social policy and caregiving (for example Croft, 1986; Dalley, 1988; Finch and Groves, 1980, 1983; Gibson and Allen, 1989; Pascall, 1986; Williams, 1989) lies in their challenge to the conventional construction of family and gender in social policy and in particular their elaboration of the need for integration of the dual surface of the hitherto privatized domain of the home and the public arena across which these analyses must move. Importantly, the feminist perspective has emphasized the exploitative relationship between the carer and the state and opened for scrutiny contradictions within the notion of 'care' by identifying the oppositional character of 'taking charge' and 'feeling concern' (Graham, 1983), and of affection and physical management and work in contrast to its delineation as intuitive and essentialist.

My position is that the complexities of power relations and ideologies are identified within the feminist researcher/researched relationship because a major feminist objective has been to 'undermin[e] existing conventions of representations' (Felski, 1989: 31). Although feminist researchers have questioned many aspects of the construction and management of these relationships within mainstream social-science research, there is a need for further, more reflexive analysis to avoid textual appropriation of the researched; and to focus attention on difference as a means of more fully representing the complexities of the social world. Where issues of social policy are concerned, it becomes all the more necessary as Statham *et al.* have stated, that these policies, often 'formulated on the macrosocial level' should 'translate effectively on the microlevel of individual and group experience' (1988: 4). Avoiding appropriation and highlighting difference are crucial means by which a researcher may empower participants in her research. Following discussion of an example from interview data from the REACH study, I will consider in more detail the implications of appropriation in social research and propose some research strategies which more adequately attend to feminist researchers' concerns for empowerment of the participants in that research.

The interview text

In many respects, the texts of informal caregivers participating in my research, i.e., spouses and adult children, represent caring as work and as destructive of personal relationships, and confirm feminist readings of the exploitation of family obligation by the health system. Because of the degree of stress under which these caregivers laboured it is easy to respond to the material primarily on that basis and highlight the exploitative nature of the role. But interspersed through a number of texts are different moments which speak of love and affection and regard, which mitigate temporarily the tensions of the role, and which disrupt and qualify the subjective experience of exploitation. These moments by no means negate that reading but they indicate points of complication and of contradiction which the analysis must additionally identify and explain.

These moments are, significantly, very largely restricted to the spouses' texts rather than those of the adult children. Quantitatively speaking, even in the spouses' texts, these alternative affectionate moments pale into insignificance in relation to the accounts of the stress and monotony of the everyday. Yet it is these brief and ambiguously positioned moments that allow caregivers to reaffirm the value of their role. One 71-year-old woman, whose voice throughout our two interviews was very flat, tired and slow, said:

> Well, as I say, um, my husband is happy at home and I am happy to have
> him at home . . . and I feel that . . . once he went away perhaps it wouldn't

be the same and I think he's getting to that stage now that perhaps if he went away as long as he was fed and looked after, it wouldn't really matter.

She begins with a strong statement of her intentions and her perceptions of her husband's well-being then suddenly moves off in an unexpected direction. After having stated that joint happiness as sufficient reason for her husband to stay at home, her first clause in the second line breaks her line of thought and turns the emotional content on its head. Her *raison d'être* for her role (her husband's happiness) which seemed secure in her opening words is suddenly cast into doubt.

My reading of this quotation is that her satisfaction with her role, with all its very real trials and tribulations, depends on the extent of her husband's cognitive awareness and thus on his ability to discriminate. What becomes difficult for her is the point at which she has to take account of the possibility that it is not just a question of whether he would be unhappy in continuing care, but when he would no longer be able to discriminate between the two environments and (very pertinently) no longer discriminate between her personal care and that given by another. She returned to the subject later:

> *Sometimes* I think to myself, 'Well, you know, if you were in hospital, I don't think that it would make much difference. I don't think you'd . . . *really care* as long as you . . . were being fed . . and looked after', and then I think, '*Well*, I don't know. Why would you put your arm around me at night, if you didn't know that it wasn't me?' And I always said, 'Well, as soon as he forgets who I am', but I don't really think that he has ever . . . because – now the other night he tried to wake me up. . . I was awake, but I thought, 'I won't say too much' . . . and then he said, 'Dear' . . . Then he said it again . . . and I thought, 'Oh, I had better say something', so I answered. Oh, but before I did, he said . . . 'It's your husband, Steve, talking', so I thought, 'Oh, I had better come to' and . . . So I thought, 'Well, you know, he can't have forgotten who I am'.

Here her doubts have become more substantial ('*sometimes*', '*really care*') about whether her husband should be institutionalised. She appears to be making a more definite and despondent movement towards deciding for hospital care. Her words indicate recognition of *her* increasing absence from her husband's world. But this movement towards an acceptance of institutionalization is arrested, initially by her reading of his placing his arm around her as confirming his presence and his validation of her as *known* and then by the poignant event of his speaking, all the more so because his speech has almost entirely gone. A sentence such as 'It's your husband, Steve, talking' represents for her a triumph of determination to assert himself and their relationship. It allows her to reaffirm the point of her personal sacrifices, that she is still remembered, that their joint life has meaning – which itself then indicates a complex *interdependent* relationship.

Extracts such as this one derive their significance from the hesitation, contradictoriness and recursiveness of the spoken voice (Barthes, 1973) and because of the light they cast on the painful moving across the surfaces of remembrance/nonremembrance, presence/absence. They also point to the significance of events about which little was said but which were crucial especially to an appreciation of the elderly spouses' experience of caregiving and to their ability and desire to sustain their role. Furthermore, they raise important questions about the weight that sociology has traditionally assigned to data which occurs only momentarily because of its deeply engrained valorizing of quantity.

In relation to developing fuller representations of caring, the tension arising from the duality of positioning (willing/exploited) has to be simultaneously maintained so that women (and men) who derive significant positive affectional and personal meaning from their role are not defined as imbued with 'false consciousness' as Croft has noted (1986: 24). The disjunction between the experiential (where caring is not always defined as exploitative) and ideology (where it is) should not only be remarked but incorporated into the analysis. Rather than representing the caring body as uniformly (monolithically) exploited or alternatively uniformly (monolithically) willing, the data from my research suggests that its constituents are unstable and are differently constituted by, for example, generational positioning, age, gender, ideology, prior experience of acting as a caregiver, the past and current relationship with the elderly person, and ability to command resources (Opie, 1990a). All these different dimensions require elaboration. Furthermore, part of the representation of that body requires the exploration of the manner and extent of 'tactics' of resistance to the role (de Certeau, 1984: xix) and the elaboration of the degree to which the body is more or less fully inscribed in a particular micropolitics of power focused around only one orientation to caring.

Appropriation is a term which conventionally defines social relations in terms of power relations. More recently, and notably in the work of Edward Said (1978, 1989), the critical importance of textual representation in the work of appropriation has been demonstrated. Although Said has concentrated upon the relations of colonizer and colonized in his analysis, his argument is very informative for research on the elderly because the characteristic features of the colonizer/colonized relationship are clearly replicated in the relationship of health system/informal caregiver and researcher/researched.

Appropriation of the 'other'

Said (1978) defines 'appropriation' as the means by which the experiences of the 'colonized' (a term used to link those colonized in the imperialistic sense of the word and those 'located in zones of dependency and peripherality' (Said, 1989: 207)) are interpreted by a (more)

dominant group to sustain a particular representation or view of the
'other' as part of an ideological stance. This practice is complex,
interlocking, self-fulfilling and constraining. Reference by writers to
other literature in the field designates that literature as authoritative
and allows them to gain from that textual authority. Adopting a
Foucauldian stance, Said argues that language cannot be regarded as a
transparent, truthful medium through which the world is simply
apprehended as it is but, instead, that it is fully implicated in power
relations.

He identifies two ways by which textual authority is constituted.
The first he calls 'strategic location' which defines the location of the
author in relation to the material about which she writes; and the
second is a process called 'strategic formation' which defines how texts
acquire 'mass, density, and referential power among themselves and
thereafter in the culture at large' (20). Arguing that the author's
location is indicated by the narrative voice adopted, by structure,
images, themes and motifs, he goes on to critique, within the historical
development of the discipline of Orientalism, the notion of scholarship
as facilitating the development of new knowledge. He suggests instead
that the affiliation of each work to others within the field increases its
own referential power and equally disguises its own modes of representation; and within that process of reference and representation, the
impact of the novel is reduced by a series of comparisons between the
new and the familiar. This is achieved through a filtering of the new
through the old so that the new is suppressed in favour of the old; and
the potentially destabilizing impact of new knowledge is subverted by a
process which permits the established view to retain its dominance.[2]
This continual mediation of interpretative attitudes, where each builds
upon and sustains the authoritative position of self and others in the
same field, leads to a situation where

> knowledge no longer requires application to reality; knowledge is what
> gets passed on, silently, without comment, from one text to another . . .
> what matters is that [ideas] are *there*, to be repeated, echoed and
> re-echoed uncritically (Said, 1978: 116).

so that

> each individual contribution first causes changes within the field and then
> promotes a new stability in a way that on a surface covered with twenty
> compasses the introduction of the twenty-first will cause all the others to
> quiver, and then settle into a new accommodating configuration (273).

Said's description of the process of generating and transmitting
knowledge is as applicable in the conduct of research in the social
sciences as it is to cultural relations. Feminist social research needs to
be highly aware of the potential for appropriation which accompanies
the researcher's ideological positioning and that initiating a new

'strategic form' within a research field implies modifying the 'strategic location' of the researcher. If one accepts Briggs's (1986) argument that all data is inherently unstable, how much is this instability and the otherness of the participants fully acknowledged in the research report and therefore recognized as affecting any conclusions? What does it mean to write critically but less authoritatively when the act of writing is so strongly associated with authority and centrality? The force of Said's argument is that developing new knowledge in an established field requires modifying the conventional textual practices in that field particularly as those practices constitute a colonizing or appropriative relationship between the researcher and the participants in the research. What this means is that the problem of appropriation and its solution lie within the researcher's way of working with the texts produced by that research; in other words, by the researcher's textual practice.

Textual practices

In this section I want to discuss the contribution of deconstructive textual practice to the reduction of appropriation. I suggest that this can be made across several planes through: (1) an identification of the constraints ideology can impose on data; (2) the indirect empowerment of participants by writing texts which represent a range of positionings within the field under investigation; and (3) a discussion of ways in which interpretive control can be shared between researcher and participants.

My discussion of the significance of a deconstructive reading of participants' texts is premised on research practice which is closed to more quantitative modes of working. A deconstructive analysis requires the detailed accessing of the participant's world. It depends on the taping and full transcription of interviews which, although 'unstructured', generate their own coherence through their responsiveness to the concerns of the participant. The researcher, in the analysis and writing of her text, is engaged in a fluid process of identifying and questioning ideology (her own, not merely the other's), her location within the literature, the nature of her textual practice and the personal and political implications of methodology for the participants in the study.

What I am suggesting is that a deconstructive reading may mitigate the issues of authority and ideological appropriation which Said has identified, but never entirely overcome them because of the impossibility of avoiding suppression or of writing beyond ideology (Threadgold, 1986). Mitigation is possible because a deconstructive reading does not attempt to be definitive. In order to maximize a non-appropriable stance towards participants the writer of a deconstructive sociological text should be explicit about its limitations and the implications of participants' locations (including the writer's). Further-more, the writer should consciously attempt to move away from a uniform textual surface, which represents only the researcher's voice, to the creation of a report which is more fissured, that is, one in which different and often competing voices within a society are recognized. Nor is it sufficient to posit one's ideological position. It is necessary, I believe, to continually re-examine the extent to which that ideology contributes to a failure to see beyond it, and to question particular truths which adhere to it and the stereotypes which develop from it.

As (partial) alternatives to Said's representation of conventional academic research as characterized by textual closure and appropri-ation I have identified four practices assisting in the creation of differently structured texts. These alternative practices, which make available the evidence on which one's interpretations are based and which attempt to move beyond the 'subject-become-object' status of the participant in relation to the researcher, are: (i) recognition of the limitations of the researcher's research and knowledge; (ii) the analytic reading of the participants' texts; (iii) some principles in relation to the incorporation of quotations from the participants' texts – what I am calling here the 'writing in of voices'; and (iv) issues of empowerment.

Limitations of research and knowledge

In a discussion of the nature of ethnographic research, Clifford displaces the ethnographer to a position 'at the edge of the frame' (1986: 1), a felicitous phrase which undermines the authoritativeness of the re-search and introduces elements of incompleteness and contingency. Historically, however, Clifford argues that anthropological (and socio-logical) studies have disguised their inherent limitations, claiming instead an ability to portray what he describes as the 'essence' (Clifford, 1983: 124ff) of the society through the use of various devices or textual strategies. One such device was an emphasis on observation which allowed the ethnographer, through a typifying procedure, to record characteristic behaviours and cultural ceremonies; another, the use of 'powerful abstractions' which enabled ethnographers to assert their possession of the 'heart' of the culture (125). Such practices go together with the conviction that true statements about another culture can be made. They serve to validate the representation of the other culture, which it is the task of the ethnographer's text to produce, yet work to conceal the fact, as Said (1978: 273) notes, that all representations are 'implicated, intertwined, embedded, interwoven with a great many other things besides the "truth" which is itself a representation', being 'embedded first in the language and then in the culture, institutions and political ambience of the representer'.

Yet to present one's research outcomes as contingent and incom-plete goes against very strong Western notions of objectivity and truth and raises questions about the authority of texts and modes of writing in which limitations are overtly acknowledged. Taking up a strategic location 'at the edge of the frame' has fundamental implications for the practice of social research.

The analytic reading

A deconstructive or postmodernist reading is a distinctive mode of reading and interpretation of textual data. It is constituted by attention to the paradoxical, the contradictory, the marginal, and by the foregrounding (not suppression) of these elements. Its focus on difference and on marginality within a text means that it specifically attends to what may be quantifiably insignificant but whose (remarked) presence may question a more conventional interpretation and expand theoretical understanding. It demands reflexivity from researchers and a challenge to their ideological positions from the data may be recognized. It accepts that the research report is limited in its representation of actuality, despite its apparent fullness, a point made emphatically by Barthes whose characterization of representation as 'deformation' (Said, 1978: 273) emphasises the selectivity and incompleteness of any account.

Writing in voices

Following postmodernist theory I have argued for the production of texts which incorporate multiple voices, citing its value for theory and the empowerment of participants (Opie, 1988a (especially Chapters 2 and 3) and b). Such a practice, however, raises at least three issues: (1) the criteria for the selection of quotations; (2) the question whether including extracts from interviews is a sufficient means of weaving other voices into the research report; and (3) the question whether the researcher should be solely responsible for the interpretation.

Selection of quotations

Because qualitative research often involves the analysis of thousands of lines of transcripts, principles for selection of quotations must be defined. The principles underpinning a deconstructive analysis depend upon thinking of language as nontransparent, as deeply involved in ideology, paradox, contradiction and ephemerality. The researcher must attend not only to the content of the texts of the interviews but also their textual features which may affect the reception and representation of that content because of their contribution to the interpretation.

The principles (which I am not claiming are exhaustive) that I have identified as augmenting the common practice in social research of illustrative quotation are:

The intensity of the speaking voice

I rely heavily on an aural recollection of passages since recalling or re-hearing the intensity with which a point is spoken can significantly influence the analysis. During my research on shared parenting or joint custody after separation or divorce (Opie, 1988a) one woman, in talking about how she arrived at the decision to try shared parenting, said in a rather matter of fact voice, 'I knew what I wanted'. She then launched into a page and a half of an intense and very detailed account of what *'I didn't want'*, repeating this clause persistently. The emphasis and intensity with which she spoke in addition to the content of her speech focused the issues of power in the decision-making process and the extent to which the women in the study had been responsible for the decision. This contributed to a gender analysis of power and to the recognition of the paradox of women acting traditionally in taking responsibility for the children, yet radically in that the mode of custody they chose was potentially destabilizing of traditional gender roles within the family.

The contradictory moment

There will be times when speakers, often apparently without any sign of awareness, contradict themselves in mid-sentence. On other occasions, the actual moment of contradiction is not so closely positioned. My understanding of the importance of an awareness of contradiction is located in a philosophical reading of self and identity. Acknowledgement of contradiction challenges the notion of rationality, affirms instead a much more unstable, decentred notion of self and calls for the representation of this self within the written text. Thus Close (1989: 5) for example, may write that the '*best* (or sociologically) the most relevant and rewarding way of defining 'contradiction' is: the occurrence of the simultaneous affirmation (support) and negation (denial) of an issue', but fail to explore how that occurrence can be made to make sense in a research report. A frequent sociological practice is to valorize one side or element of the contradiction, a device like those Clifford has identified, which serves to make the contradiction disappear rather than encourages the discovery of the ground 'in between' (Poovey, quoting Derrida, 1988: 53).

Emotional content or tone

The emotional content of the voice contributes significantly to the implications of what is said. To illustrate this I want to take two extracts from the texts of two elderly male carers. Both are talking about the frustration they experience and the difficulties of coming to terms with their spouse's memory loss and increasingly erratic behaviour. One man said:

> If I go out of the house she's stumbling around and she picks up these files, somebody's papers or something, and . . . she is liable to pick up somebody's pile and ahh . . . you know . . . put them down somewhere or other. (*Voice becomes increasingly loud and angry*) 'Now where's that pile I was looking at – I was working at it!' (*Adopts shriller voice to represent wife's voice*) 'I haven't done anything with it. I haven't touched it' (*Louder as self*) 'How often do I have to tell you to *leave my bloody stuff alone*! That's not my stuff. It's client's stuff!' . . . I said, 'I'm not having trouble with clients just because this stupid wife of mine has shifted stuff! (*Voice grows angrier*) 'Now will you leave that stuff alone!! Look, I have just told you (*slams desk*) Leave that stuff alone.' (*Whispers*) It's not registering. . . . I, I've realized this . . . It's no good. It's no good doing that . . . . I've just got to say, (*In calm even voice*) 'Oh no. Don't touch it dear'. She's already forgotten that 2 minutes ago I'd grabbed the thing away from her. (*Whining voice as wife*) 'You, you are always, you are always grabbing things away from me!' (*Assumes own voice; speaking sadly*) No. No. She has already forgotten it. . . At least, I, I, I am, I am accepting. I am getting . . . It's becoming more a part of me the fact that ah . . . these things are

just *not* registering. It is no good growling at her because 2 minutes later she does the same thing *again*!

The other man says in a voice that remains patient, albeit slightly bemused and bewildered throughout:

> **Participant:** She's got a blue toothbrush. I said, 'Leave it on the basin.'
> **AO:** What, rather than hang it up in a cupboard?
> **Participant:** Yeah. Oh, she'll never find it. And then she'll come out and say, 'Where's my toothbrush? Is this it?' Now then she'll come out with the toothpaste, and say, 'Is this what I use?' Without the toothbrush. So muddled up.
> **AO:** How's that for you? Is that the point where you begin to feel irritated and frustrated?
> **Participant:** Frustrated . . . [*mumbling*]. Christ, the other night she comes out with my toothbrush. I said, 'You know that's not yours. Mine's red and your's is blue.' Five minutes later she's off saying, 'Where's my toothbrush, is this it?' I said, 'If you ask me again I'll scream.' You know. That sort of thing. And you think after all you're being a bit tough. But, um . . . It's those things that rattle you.

Without going into a full analysis of the differences, it is sufficient to note the vast gap between the two men's manner of speaking, contrasting the predominant anger, rage and slide into guilt of the first speaker with the gentleness and concern and exasperation of the second. Moreover, this difference in approach reflects personality, prior experience in caregiving and domestic work before their spouses became demented; and it highlights significantly the different nature of their (male) experiences as carers. A concentration on the differences in emotion between the speakers assists in a finely grained analysis of carers' experiences. It contributes, too, to a more complex gender analysis (Jacobus, 1986), since intertextual comparisons between elderly carers' texts in tone and emotional content indicate points at which male and female carers cross gender-specific boundaries. Furthermore, it suggests that specific verbal content, such as the repeated denigratory comments about the demented person (as well as the abusive emotional content) may help in identifying situations of potential psychological and physical abuse.

The extent to which the participant uses whole sentences, rather than the more usual recursive speech patterns

Conversational speech is marked by redundancy, repetitiveness and incompleteness and depends extensively on the listener's ability to interpret a range of nonverbal communicative features. Under these circumstances the use of a nonredundant mode of speech is extremely powerful (Barthes, 1973/86). Focusing on the non-redundant speech act may assist in the identification of a particular ideological moment, inform the readers of the manner in which issues of power and control affect the process of data collection and indicate the unstable ground of the researcher/researched relationship (Opie, 1988b).

The identification of examples of these four points in interview texts relies on a close textual reading and the inclusion by the transcriber of some of the characteristics of the spoken word – sudden movements of emphasis, breaks in a sentence and changes of direction, and movement through a range of emotions. One of the implications of such speech behaviour is that the reproduction of the voice only in a transcript of the word spoken is inadequate and that a more powerful means of presentation should be found so that the voice actually speaking may be evidenced within the text. What is fascinating in thinking about this is that it implies a revision of procedures and assumptions about written texts which have developed over a long period. For example Ginzburg (1983: 93) observes:

> We know that textual criticism evolved . . . with the writing around Homeric poems, and developed further . . . when classical scholars improved on the first hastily printed editions of the classics. First, the elements which related to voice and gesture were discarded as redundant . . . The result has been a progressive dematerialization, or refinement, of texts, a process in which the appeal of the original to our various senses has been purged away.

Including extracts from transcripts aurally as well as visually within a research report is surely not a complicated technical process. However, such a practice could make it much easier to identify participants and so require a careful process of consent as well as discussion about what sections of the transcript were to be available for direct quotation.

The control of the interpretation
Recently, the practice has developed, particularly among anthropologists, of giving a draft of a report to research participants and asking them to comment on its validity. The point of this practice is to realign the balance of power in the research relationship by minimizing appropriation through a deliberate attempt to avoid misrepresentation and stereotype and by the expansion of the researcher's appreciation of the situation as a result of discussing and reworking the text with the participants. However, I am unclear how agreement over the final version is reached when there is more than one participant. If agreement cannot be reached, one course of action is that the contentious material is removed; another, that the interpretation of some of the participants is privileged. However, I believe the situation to be more complicated. Removal of the material does not permit it to be discussed; while subordination of one reading raises several problems.

The problematic areas are located in: (i) the implied claim that there is a final or 'deep' truth which research can reveal; (ii) the notion of 'consensus' when the processes of how consensus has been achieved and whose account privileged are left unexplored with the result that it is assumed that the participant's group is speaking in a united voice; (iii) the implications for interpretation of the different perspectives of the researcher and the researched; and (iv) the nature and/or physical appearance of the final text.

Because a postmodernist analysis highlights competing voices and raises critical appreciation of the presence of ideologies within a text, accepting an interpretation which implies a single or unified represen- tation of an event is problematic, especially since this implies that all participants are similarly located. A further implication, that partici- pants and researchers occupy an identical relationship to the data, is also problematic since participants may occupy a less analytic and more descriptive position, while researchers may be more aware of alterna- tive interpretations.

Although anthropologists have suggested (Clifford, 1983, 1986) that a co-authorship relationship with respondents should be developed or have achieved this mode of working relationship (Mbilinyi, 1989), such a relationship is difficult to achieve when participants, while constituting a community of interest, do not form a close-knit physical community. For instance, it is impossible to develop a co-authorial relationship with the informal carers whom I have interviewed because of their geographical spread and the difficulty in attending drafting meetings because of the elder's need for supervision.

The physical appearance of texts which reflect difference and seek to avoid textual smoothness have generated little comment. One example, however, is Benterrak, Muecke and Roe's (1984) *Reading the Country* in which three very different visual and physically structured texts co-exist, each representing alternative modes of reading, each claiming very different genealogies. The writerly intention, then, is not necessarily to achieve a consensus but to highlight the points of difference and the tensions between competing accounts as well as shared interpretations. Addressing difference would create a much more broken and fissured text and would focus much more attention on the nature of the interpretive processes. It would also have the effect of highlighting the sociological and ideological locations of those involved – not merely differences between the researcher and the participants, but also differences between the participants themselves and the impli- cations of location on interpretation (Rosaldo, 1986). The consequences of such practices would reinforce the significance of textuality as an integral part of research, indicate the instability of (sociological) knowledge, and challenge 'strateg[ies] of authority' (Clifford, 1983: 120).

Empowerment
I want to move now from the means of diminishing textual appropri- ation to look at more direct means of empowerment through research design and the researcher's assumptions about some of the purposes of research. I have chosen to address more the personal benefit to participants (while also noting how the ramifications spread beyond the individual) because I do not think that this area has been discussed extensively whereas the reduction of women's subordination (a domi- nant political objective of feminist scholarship) and the significance of the analytic frameworks to achieve this end have received considerable attention.

Finally, I focus on strategies and research design specifically intended to empower participants and discuss problems within feminist action-oriented research in which unacknowledged appropriative tendencies can be located. I suggest that disempowerment is located within textual appropriation. This appropriation can be partially avoided by the use of qualitative research methods which can lead to an empowerment of participants on a personal and broadly therapeutic plane. Deconstructive textual practice can importantly assist in political empowerment, through the incorporation in published research of participants' multiple and very different voices, so that the way that ideology can smooth over differences is disrupted and questioned; and through the encouragement, as a result of participation in the research, of individual and collective challenging of the system.

The private dimension of research
There are at least three ways in which a participant may be individually empowered through participation in a research project where the style of interviewing is not hindered by rigid interview schedules, and where points of specific interest can be followed in detail. I suggest that this mode of unstructured and responsive interviewing, when used reflexively, can enable especially the socially marginalized (Said's 'colonized') to be empowered because it assumes they can contribute significantly to the description and analysis of a social issue; and indeed, nearly every participant in my caregiving study agreed to take part because of their desire to help others through making their experience available and through their critique of the health system. By taking part in the research they lifted the veil of invisibility surrounding carers' everyday lives, and the experience of marginality from their existence (by becoming 'centre' even if briefly), thus opening what is generally a socially obscured experience to a more public gaze.

Because the interviews were responsive to individual preoccupations, there was an in-built therapeutic dimension to the process which I would also characterize as empowering. Some participants were able to reflect on and re-evaluate their experience as part of the process of being interviewed. For some, this re-evaluation had important personal as well as political consequences. For instance, two unmarried daughters began to question the assumptions they had hitherto made about their obligations to care unceasingly and the extent to which it was legitimate for them to 'lose' and 'sacrifice my life', and make a start in defining the point when their caring responsibilities should end.

When qualitative research incorporates the voices of marginal and hence previously silenced groups into the text it can become subversive along a number of fronts. For example, the texts of the interviews with the caregivers' challenge the ascription of caring as intuitive, affirm the existence of a world which is emotionally extraordinarily complex and contradictory, and indicate that caring is constituted within several affective positions within the field of caring, none of which are peculiar to a particular kin relationship and where the positioning of the individual carer is likely to change over time (Opie, 1990a). My interpretation of these texts, then, confirms much of the feminist critique of caring, but demonstrates aspects of that critique requiring further theorizing.

The praxis dimension of research
The final question I want to pose is: does the researcher's adoption of a praxis orientation (Ortner, 1984; Smith, 1987) avoid appropriation and support the political empowerment of the inevitably objectified 'subject', or is it merely a 'reductively pragmatic response', where practice is viewed as if it 'were a domain of actuality unencumbered by agents, interests, and contentions' (Said, 1989: 211)?

Lather's work (1986, 1988) can be read as an exemplar of an overtly political model of feminist research practice which valorizes research leading to collective social action. Her model of research has some similarities to my concept of a significant research methodology. She embraces firmly a praxis/empowerment/reciprocity paradigm, where she affirms the need to expand the knowledge base through the problemization of what is taken for granted through nondogmatic, grounded research into the mundane lives of the dispossessed. She quotes Heron to the effect that the ability of the dispossessed to 'participate in decisions that claim to generate knowledge about them' (1986: 262) avoids their manipulation. She argues that reciprocity, achieved through interactive, sequential interviewing and a negotiation of meaning through sharing of drafts, helps 'participants to understand and change their situations' (263). She also refers approvingly to a number of praxis-oriented research projects that resulted in women being able to set up organizations or centres which addressed their previously unmet and unrecognized needs. So far, so good. However, there are three points where I think her approach is open to question.

On a number of occasions Lather makes reference to the concept of 'false consciousness' which she defines (1986: 264) as a 'denial of how our commonsense ways of looking at the world are permeated with meanings that sustain our disempowerment'; she further suggests that one of the main purposes of research is to assist participants in self-reflection and understanding (her words) or self-criticism (my words). A full appreciation of false consciousness among participants is achieved by running groups for the women whom one is researching with the implication that they can be helped on from their false, to a true, state of consciousness. This is to be achieved by engaging in an 'ideology critique', the purpose being to create conditions where a questioning of beliefs, authority and culture hitherto taken for granted becomes possible and where the 'researcher joins the participants in a theoretically guided program of action' (268).

One of the difficulties about taking a critical approach to Lather's work is its current political correctness; for example, the research projects which she cites as leading to a praxis outcome include the establishment of Rape Crisis Centres. My argument is not about the outcome, but with the positioning of the various women in the research process. My discomfort with her argument derives from: (i) her failure to recognize her own processes of appropriation; (ii) her failure to treat women as other than a generic whole; and (iii) a lack of reflexivity in her research paradigm. Let me expand on these points. Critical enquiry, as Lather defines it, is that which, in a complex series of interactions, begins as a response to the experiences and desires of the oppressed. The researcher guides the dispossessed in 'a process of cultural transformation', itself a mutually educative process where the researcher and the researched both contribute to the expansion of the other's knowledge – a process whereby the respondents are liberated from 'ideologically frozen understandings' (Lather: 1986: 268) and become aware that these no longer serve their interests. During the period of the research, the critical researcher submits her work to participants for their evaluation of its accuracy but at the same time must have reference beyond their assessments because of the contamination of 'false consciousness' (269) and must then negotiate meanings with the participants *without becoming impositional* (269; Lather's italics).

What concerns me is that there is a considerable tension between her intention to liberate women and her failure to recognize her own ideological location (however positively valued that may currently be) which is itself taken for granted and is therefore seen as true, rather than apprehended as ideological. I think that the assumption of correctness introduces a further tension between all participants. There is a pretence of equality where the researched are understood to have some knowledge not yet possessed/appropriated by the researcher (but the superiority of some of that knowledge is not affirmed by Lather since, ultimately, the researcher is guide). The researcher is consistently privileged, particularly through her location in a more ideologically correct position – in terms of Said's concept of the colonized it could be argued that she has missionary status (with all of its unfortunate and well-meaning connotations) – thus raising doubts about the extent of the mutually transformative process that has been promised, a doubt compounded by the admission at the end that the participants' viewpoint cannot be completely relied on and that further external evidence must be sought, which one presumes will offer a higher degree of reliability.

This notion of research, then, appears to me also to disempower participants (even if differently) as do the research paradigms it seeks to displace. The object is apprehended through a particular predetermined textual attitude, the adherence to which may preclude the possibility of modification through interaction between knowledge and theory. There appears, in this somewhat rigid practice, to be less room, on the researcher's part, for reflexivity and for change; for a recognition that a single ideological position may deny and distort the experience of some women while validating that of others. We cannot engage in research divested of ideology. We can come with an overt consciousness of ideology and an awareness that all ideology can obscure as well as enlighten. Appropriation of the other can therefore be minimized by a constant, sensitive reflection on the way that the texts of the participants are created by ideology and yet at some points challenge it.

Conclusion

I have argued throughout this paper that textual appropriation of the other is an inevitable consequence of research. I have demonstrated that a qualitative, deconstructive, theoretical and methodological approach with its emphasis on a close textual reading can counterbalance (although by no means eliminate) this inevitability. I have suggested that this is because it facilitates the researcher's entry into complex, recursive and contradictory worlds, and because of its potential for empowerment of the participants. To return to Said's distinction which I introduced at the beginning of this paper: How do we as social researchers understand our 'strategic location' with respect to the participants in our research, and how do we define the 'strategic formation' within which we think and research? I have argued that qualitative research using a deconstructive methodology permits a more reflexive, flexible understanding of our location and it obviously introduces a new 'strategic formation' for sociological research. In particular, it helps focus fundamental questions in a new way: Who are we writing for? What kinds of authority should we claim for our texts? What kind of texts should we be producing?

Notes

Anne Opie holds a post-doctoral fellowship in the Department of Sociology and Social Work at Victoria University, Wellington, New Zealand. She is currently completing a qualitative study into the everyday experiences of informal family caregivers looking after the confused elderly.

1 For a more detailed account of the REACH research (Research with Elders and Carers at Home) see Opie (1990b). This research has been funded by the New Zealand University Grants Committee and supported by additional grants from the Internal Research Committee of Victoria University of Wellington.
2 See also Barthes's (1971/86) comments on issues of textual authority.

References

BARTHES, Roland (1971/1986) 'From work to text' in *The Rustle of Language* trans. by Richard Howard, New York: Hill & Wang.
—— (1973/1986) 'The war of language' in *The Rustle of Language* trans. by Richard Howard, New York: Hill & Wang.
BENTERRAK, Kim, MUECKE, Stephen and ROE, Paddy (1984) *Reading the Country: Introduction to Nomadology* Fremantle: Fremantle Arts Centre Press.

BRIGGS, Charles (1986) *Learning How to Ask: A Sociolinguistic Appraisal of the Role of the Interview in Social Science Research* Cambridge: Cambridge University Press.

CERTEAU de, Michel 1984 *The Practice of Everyday Life* trans. by Stephen Rendall, Berkeley: University of California Press.

CLIFFORD, James (1983) 'On ethnographic authority' *Representations* Vol. 1, No. 2: 118–46.

—— (1986) 'Introduction: Partial truths' in **CLIFFORD** and **MARCUS** (1986).

CLIFFORD, James and **MARCUS, George** (1986) editors, *Writing Culture: The Poetics and Politics of Ethnography* Berkeley: University of California Press.

CLOSE, Paul (1989) 'Policy, domestic labour and gender' *National Conference on Social Policy in Australia: What Future the Welfare State?*

CROFT, Suzy (1986) 'Women, caring and the recasting of need – a feminist reappraisal' *Critical Social Policy* Vol. 16: 23–39.

DALLEY, Gillian (1988) *Ideologies of Caring: Rethinking Community and Collectivism* London: Macmillan Educational Books.

ECO, Umberto and SEBEOK, Thomas (1983) *The Sign of the Three: Dupin, Holmes and Pierce* Bloomington: Indiana University Press.

FINCH, Janet and **GROVES, Dulcie** (1980) 'Community care and the family: a case for equal opportunities' *Journal of Social Policy* Vol. 9. No. 4: 487–511.

—— (1983) editors, *A Labour of Love: Women, Work and Caring* London: Routledge & Kegan Paul.

FELSKI, Rita (1989) *Beyond Feminist Aesthetics: Feminist Literature and Social Change* Cambridge, Mass: Harvard University Press.

GIBSON, Diane and **ALLEN, Judith** (1989) 'Parasitism and phallocentrism: a critique of social policy provisions for the aged' University of Queensland, Australia.

GINZBURG, Carlo (1983) 'Clues: Morelli, Freud, & Sherlock Holmes' in **ECO** and **SEBEOK** (1983).

GRAHAM, Hilary (1983) 'Caring: a labour of love' in **FINCH** and **GROVES** (1983).

JACOBUS, Mary (1986) 'Reading woman (reading)' in Mary Jacobus, *Reading Woman: Essays in Feminist Criticism* London: Methuen.

LATHER, Patti (1986) 'Research as praxis' *Harvard Educational Review* Vol. 56, No. 3: 257–77.

—— (1988) 'Feminist research perspectives on empowering research methodologies' *Women's Studies International Forum* Vol. 11, No. 6: 569–82.

MBILINYI, Marjorie (1989) '"I'd have been a man": politics and the labour process in producing personal narratives' in **PERSONAL NARRATIVES GROUP** (1989).

OPIE, Anne (1988a) *Shared Parenting in New Zealand after Separation and Divorce*, Ph.D. thesis, Wellington: Victoria University of Wellington, New Zealand.

—— (1988b) 'Moving beyond local colour: the voices of qualitative research' *Sites*, Vol. 17: 83–99.

—— (1990a) 'The instability of the caring body: gender and caregivers of the confused elderly' paper presented at the Sociological Association Conference of Aotearoa (New Zealand) Christchurch, December.

—— (1990b) 'Caring for the confused elderly at home: report on work in progress' *New Zealand Women's Studies Journal* Vol. 6, No. 1/2: 48–64.

ORTNER, Sherry (1984) 'Theory in anthropology since the sixties' *Comparative Studies in Society and History*, Vol. 26, No. 1: 126–66.

PASCALL, Gillian (1986) *Social Policy: A Feminist Analysis* London and New York: Tavistock.

PERSONAL NARRATIVES GROUP (1989) *Interpretating Women's Lives: Feminist Theory and Personal Narratives* Bloomington: Indiana University Press.

POOVEY, Mary (1988) 'Feminism and deconstruction' *Feminist Studies* Vol. 14, No. 1: 51–65.

ROSALDO, Renato (1986) 'From the door of his tent' in **CLIFFORD** and **MARCUS** (1986).

SAID, Edward (1978) *Orientalism* London: Penguin.

—— (1989) 'Representing the colonized: anthropology's interlocutors' *Critical Inquiry* Vol. 15: 205–25.

SMITH, Dorothy (1987) *The Everyday World as Problematic: A Feminist Sociology* Boston: N.E. University Press.

STATHAM, Anne, MILLER Eleanor and **MAUKSCH, Hans** (1988) editors, 'Women's approach to work: the creation of knowledge' in **STATHAM, MILLER** and **MAUKSCH** *The Worth of Women's Work: A Qualitative Synthesis* Albany: State University of New York Press.

THREADGOLD, Terry (1986) 'Semiotics – ideology – language' in **THREADGOLD, GROSZ, KRESS** and **HALLIDAY** (1986) *Language, Semiotics, Ideology* Sydney: Pathfinder Press.

WILLIAMS, Fiona (1989) *Social Policy: A Critical Introduction. Issues of Race, Gender and Class* Cambridge: Polity Press.

DISABLED WOMEN AND THE FEMINIST AGENDA

Nasa Begum

Introduction

Traditionally, there has been a tendency to view disabled people as one homogenous group with no gender distinctions. The reality of being a disabled woman and having a physical disability has to a large extent been overlooked by both the disability and feminist movements. However, there is little doubt that the dual oppression of sexism and handicapism places disabled women in an extremely marginalized position. Writing as an Asian disabled woman I want to open up a debate about the position of disabled women and demand that a concerted effort is made to ensure that our needs, wishes and aspirations are incorporated in all feminist debates. I will argue that the experiences of disabled women must be seen as an integral part of the social, economic and political structures which serve to control our daily lives. I recognize that disabled women cannot be treated as a unitary group: factors such as types of disability, race, sexuality and class will influence our individual experiences and these may differ from the experiences of other disabled women. However, it is essential that we use our common experiences to develop a political analysis which creates bonds and forges positive strengths.

By drawing together literature on disability and gender, I intend to demonstrate that the concerns of disabled women strike at the core of both the disability rights and feminist movements. After a brief analysis of the concept of disability, certain feminist tools will be used to provide an analysis of the experiences of disabled women. Particular emphasis will be given to three factors which have had a crucial role in understanding the lives of women: gender roles, self-image and sexuality.

The triple oppression of being a black disabled woman has not been overlooked. There are profound implications for those of us who experience the oppression of racism, sexism and handicapism. However, there has been very little analysis of the experiences of black disabled people, or of the diverse and complicated issues which affect us. To avoid the dangers of feeding into cultural misunderstandings and racist stereotypes, we urgently need a thorough investigation of the experiences of black disabled people. We could then develop an analysis of our position as black disabled women and articulate our particular needs. Unfortunately, it is not possible within the ambit of this article to provide this analysis, and therefore I shall suggest that all the issues affecting disabled women also apply to black disabled women. However, the way in which we experience and interpret these issues is likely to differ as the dimension of race interacts to shape our lives.

Disability: what does it mean?

It is essential to clarify at the outset exactly what is meant by the words disability and handicap. The terms used and their implicit politics within the disability rights movement are subject to ongoing debate. Throughout this article the Union of Physically Impaired Against Society (UPIAS) definition of disability will be adopted.

> Disability: the disadvantage or restriction of activity caused by a
> contemporary social organisation which takes no or little account of
> people who have physical impairments and thus excludes them from
> participation in the mainstream of social activities. Physical disability is
> therefore a particular form of social oppression. (UPIAS, 1981: 14)

The word handicap is used to describe the social ramifications of having a disability; it is not the biological condition but the societal barriers which restrict our lives as disabled people.

There are essentially two theoretical frameworks for understanding the concept of disability. The first may be described as the individualistic perspective, in which disability is interpreted as a deviation from accepted or expected notions of normality, the differentness is regarded as a personal tragedy which the individual must seek to 'come to terms with'. Stereotypes of passivity and childlike dependency are created for members of the 'disabled' and, at the same time, roles are prescribed which render us powerless. To avoid embarrassment and inconvenience to the nondisabled world, an emphasis is placed on accepting the goal of normality:

> There's a tremendous emphasis . . . to be as able-bodied as possible. It's
> like standing up is considered infinitely better than sitting down, even if
> you're standing up by standing in a total frame . . . that you can't move in,
> which hurts and takes hours to get on and off, and looks ugly.
> (Sutherland, 1981: 73)

The individual perspective of disability makes no attempt to examine the social, economic and political perspectives which influence the lives of disabled people. Therefore an alternative framework re-defining disability as a form of social oppression has been put forward by disabled people: disability is a form of social oppression which is articulated through prevailing ideological, social and political determinants and, as a consequence of these, disabled people are socially excluded and handicapism is constructed.

Disabled people as a collective force have, through the disability rights movement, used the experiences and understanding of disability as social oppression to: (a) challenge the professional and public perceptions of disability as being a natural consequence of a biological condition; and (b) demand the right to self-determination and full and equal participation in the social, economic and political sphere.

However, unless gender distinctions are dealt with as a matter of urgency, the oppression encountered by disabled women will be compounded and our powerless position will be exacerbated.

An overview of the position of disabled women

Although disability may be the predominant characteristic by which a disabled person is labelled, it is essential to recognize that gender influences play an important role in determining how that person's disability is perceived and reacted to. A frequent complaint lodged by disabled women is that rehabilitation programmes place so much emphasis on 'cultivating competitive attitudes' and addressing concerns about male sexuality, that while enabling men to aspire to dominant notions of masculinity, the needs of disabled women are ignored or left on the periphery (Morris, 1989; Matthews, 1983; Becker, 1978; and Duffy, 1981). Fine and Asch explain:

> To be male in our society is to be strong, assertive and independent; to be female is to be weak, passive and dependent, the latter conforming to the social stereotypes of the disabled. For both categories the disabled woman inherits ascriptions of passivity, and weakness. (1985: 11)

Both disability and gender are understood as socially constructed classifications, the impact of each may be mitigated or exacerbated according to whether the individual can be identified with an alternative social group which is perceived to be inferior. Disabled men could identify either with the negative role of disability, or they could strategically choose to identify with the powerful and advantageous male role. Both roles available to disabled women label us as inferior, passive and weak. Fine and Asch write:

> Disabled women are not only more likely to internalize society's rejection, but they are more likely than disabled men to identify themselves as

'disabled'. The disabled male possesses a relatively positive self-image and is more likely to identify as 'male' rather than as 'disabled'. The disabled woman appears to be more likely to introject society's rejection, and to identify as disabled. (1985: 9)

Disabled women have become perennial outsiders, our powerless position has not been seriously addressed by either the disability rights or the women's movement. This simultaneous neglect is unforgivable; the exclusion on the basis of gender or disability cannot be defended by groups which purport to express the demands of all those who are ascribed membership to them by virtue of a particular biological criterion.

Although all women are supposed to be represented in the fight for women's liberation, disabled women have drawn attention to the fact that the movement has disregarded them:

The popular view of women with disabilities has been one mixed with repugnance. Perceiving disabled women as childlike, helpless, and victimized, non-disabled feminists have severed them from the sisterhood in an effort to advance more powerful, competent and appealing female icons. (Fine and Asch, 1988: 4)

As disabled women we have spoken about how our experiences as women leave us in a marginal and ambiguous position. One woman claims: 'there is no arm of the movement concerned about disabled women . . . we do fit in, but only on the outside like some sort of mascot'. (Duffy, 1981: 167). Another woman explains, 'In the women's group I go to I am a token disabled.' (Begum, 1990).

It must not be assumed that disabled women are silent observers of feminist issues. One woman explains the contribution to be made:

Able-bodied women can learn from the disabled, who have had to learn this before they can truly cope, that the physical body is not as important as the person that lives inside; that one is first a person, and second a female; that sex is less important than these two; and that every woman who is honestly involved in her own personal growth is making a contribution to the women's movement whether she is aware of it or not. (Duffy, 1981: 168)

There are certain aspects of women's oppression which highlight the parallels and the differences between disabled women and nondisabled women. The basic issues may be the same for both groups but the impact of disability means that the implications or effects may differ. I have chosen to examine some of the areas which have played a crucial role in developing a feminist understanding of the position of women. These are gender roles, body image and sexuality, all of which help us to understand the process of socialization in our lives. The division into three distinct areas is an artificial one created for the purposes of writing; in reality our experiences in relation to gender roles, self-image and sexuality are inextricably linked; they interweave together to determine our experiences, and thus cannot be regarded as separate aspects of our lives.

Gender roles

A woman's role is traditionally one of nurturer; throughout her life she is to a large extent defined by her capacity as a daughter, wife or mother. Women have criticized the concept of the family as an oppressive institution through which socially-constructed feminine roles have been established and maintained. It can represent the power struggle between men and women in its starkest form (see Barrett and McIntosh, 1982). Despite the fact that women have fought hard to challenge traditional sex roles, the influences of such roles still remains strong and therefore their significance should not be underestimated. Graham (1983: 21) explains:

> Caring – whether for husbands and children, or for those outside the nuclear family – is far from trivial and insignificant. It is moreover, an activity where questions of success are constantly raised, and women can indeed feel 'unsexed' by failure.

For disabled women, there may be an automatic assumption that our disabilities will prevent us from ever taking up such traditionally defined roles.

To many women, the absence of rigidly prescribed gender roles would be a source of great relief and a sense of liberation, but for those of us who have been constantly denied access to what could be construed as the 'goals of womanhood', the attainment of such goals can be a real sense of achievement:

> I pushed myself to have the very things my parents said I could not have. I was determined to prove I was a 'normal' woman. I deliberately sought the most handsome man to parade around. And although I did not consciously intend to do it, I became pregnant out of wedlock at 17, which was extremely affirming for me. One of my proud moments was parading around the supermarket with my belly sticking out for all to see that I was indeed a woman, and that my body worked like a normal woman's body. (Rousso, 1978: 159)

Occupying a position in 'no woman's land' may either (a) push disabled women into choosing very traditional feminine roles to aspire to notions of 'normality'; or (b) lead disabled women to select nontraditional feminine roles as a process of default rather than personal choice. However, one must be wary of assuming that nontraditional roles are adopted as the only option available. There are some disabled women who do not wish to be confined by the prescriptions of femininity and a decision to be a single parent, a career woman, a partner in a lesbian relationship, or a lesbian mother, is a positive choice.

Women who have been married before the onset of disability often find that the perceived threat to the traditional role of wife and housekeeper can cause irreparable damage. Hannaford (1985:18) claims:

> Four times as many women as men face marital breakdown, after the onset of disability. This reflects, I think men's inability to see themselves in the role of 'carer' . . . the man usually defines this new situation as unacceptable and leaves. With the back-up that this view is 'normal', now that the woman has forfeited her right to 'normality' and hence acceptability, the man will feel remorse at his actions which are seen as justified. Under the pressure of these implicit assumptions, the woman will often agree. A negative self-image will result and her expectations and demands of life will be curtailed accordingly.

If, as disabled women, we do not conform to conventional gender roles then the fight to gain access to institutions such as the family becomes extremely difficult, if not impossible. Although these institutions are considered oppressive by many feminists, the struggle against the family may be different for those of us who are excluded from the outset.

As disabled women our experiences of institutions such as the family are significantly influenced by the pressure of conventional gender-role distinctions. We either make a positive decision for political or personal reasons not to ascribe to traditional roles, or we fight very hard to conform to the ascriptions which classify us as 'real women'. Alternatively, we recognize society's rejection, and in realizing that the socially sanctioned roles are prohibited, we acquire a sense of worthlessness and negative self-image.

Self-image

Self-image is the internal concept we have of ourselves. Our self-image as women is significantly influenced by our body-image. Indeed, for many women self-image is synonymous with body-image. This is a direct consequence of the fact that women are primarily defined by physical appearances. Body-image is determined by the messages we receive about how our bodies should look and behave. It is a gendered concept which has been constructed by men to endorse the view of women as ornamental objects put on this planet for the gratification of men. The dominant image of women does not incorporate the diverse and individual characteristics of women. Instead, it suggests that an attractive woman is young, medium height, slim, nondisabled and white. Consequently, black women, older women, fat women, too short or too tall women and disabled women are not attractive because they do not conform to the dominant body-image in Western society.

The term 'disabled women' can quickly and easily be substituted with the words 'defective women'. In a society which places substantial emphasis on 'feminine' attractiveness and the ability to take care of one's own basic bodily functions, disabled women are dealt a severe blow. One disabled woman writes, 'I had this image of myself as a big blob, no shape just dead meat' (Carillo, *et al.*, 1982: 26).

Disabled women live in bodies which do not always work and often defy the dominant notion of 'normal' appearance. This can be particularly difficult to reconcile with the pervasive myth of perfection:

> I try hard to accept my body and improve on it but it's a losing battle. I'm bombarded with pictures of beautiful bodies and I just cannot compete, so I try to hide my flaws (Morris, 1989: 61)

Through the countless images of beauty that find their way into the daily lives of women, the message that they must have a certain appearance to be admired and loved, particularly by men, is internalized. Certain aspects of disability can make it difficult for a woman to incorporate her physical characteristics and her daily needs into this concept of attractiveness:

> Most disabilities come equipped with drooping breasts, a thin rib cage and a lax-tum, due to a lack of muscle . . . The inability of the disabled person to be purely physical, showing body movement, posture . . . can be a great disadvantage within the 'market place' of relationships. (Campling, 1981: 17)

> I did feel less sexually attractive, because I was surrounded by metal and wheels and had no control over my body, bladder and bowels. I needed help with absolutely everything and couldn't see how men could find me sexually attractive. (Morris, 1989: 82)

In view of the fact that disabled women may challenge societal perceptions of accepted, or expected, standards of appearance, our differences may be labelled as 'defects':

> Specialists trained to treat one or other of our body parts have contributed to our dismembered body image. Value judgements are assigned to our 'good' parts and 'bad' parts. Health is seen as a virtue, disease as evil and ugly. (Browne *et al.*, 1985: 246).

With very little attention given to the positive aspects of a person's appearance and a tendency to reduce the body to an asexual object, disabled women learn very early on that their bodies can be objects which are manipulated and controlled by others (Boston Women's Health Book Collective, 1984).

> Having a disability made me very aware at an early age of the messages I was receiving from the larger society about how I was supposed to look and how you're supposed to be. Also as the doctors poked and studied me endlessly, I learnt more quickly than some non-disabled women that I'm seen as an object. . . . I was made to walk naked . . . and then lie on a mat while in turn they (5 male student doctors) examined my body, opening and closing my legs, poking and prodding here and there and making comments. I was at the age when I was developing from a child into a woman . . . I started to lose my self-respect. (Campling, 1981: 10).

If a woman loses respect for her own body, and internalizes the negative messages that hang the label 'defective and undesirable' around her neck, then it is not surprising that her body becomes a source of pain, embarrassment and guilt. This can subsequently lead her to believing that her body is the enemy and she has no control over it:

> One of the results of considering your body to be the enemy is a sort of disassociation. The disassociation manifests itself in a feeling of not owning one's body because it is causing so much trouble. It may happen that someone else is spending a lot of time taking care of it, so it is really easy to just hand it over to that person. Consequently we see a mind-body split which has major implications for self-concept and sexuality. (Bogle *et al.*, 1981: 92)

Body-image has a profound impact on the way in which we perceive ourselves. A positive body-image can help to build confidence and promote self-esteem, and a negative image can affirm feelings of inferiority, worthlessness and inadequacies.

Sexuality

Sexuality refers to the whole span of personality related to sexual behaviour. To challenge male supremacy and object to the sexual objectification of women by men, the women's movement has demanded the right for women to define their own sexuality and an end to all discrimination against lesbians. Disabled women are entitled to the same rights as other women, however we may be a long way behind in trying to reach the same goals. One woman explains the dilemma she faces by saying:

> It has been rare in my life that I have feared men getting sexual with me, because most men don't see me as a sex object in the same way as they see most women for THAT I am profoundly grateful! . . . But if only more women had made me feel like a woman. (Campling, 1981: 32)

Until recently, disabled people have been seen as asexual. The non-disabled world has found it difficult to grapple with the idea that these 'damaged' bodies could have sexual feelings, the mere thought that they may engage in sexual behaviour is considered 'unwholesome, repulsive and comical' (Greengross, 1976: 2).

Usually, during adolescence children develop an understanding of their own sexuality and anticipate or explore relationships with others. Body-image and self-esteem often significantly influence a child's sexual development. For a disabled daughter who has acquired a negative self-concept, the control and manipulation of her body by others may leave her feeling ambivalent and confused about her own sexuality. One woman talks about her turmoil: 'It was difficult enough to be feeling so confused about my sexual identity. Not to be able to experiment with boys only added to my confusion and growing self-doubts.' (Rousso, 1978: 146).

Despite the moves to push for the recognition of women's sexual needs, there is still a notion that the disabled woman's needs are either nonexistent or inferior. One young adolescent woman with spina bifida who asked her gynaecologist whether she would be able to have satisfying sexual relations received the following response, 'Don't worry honey, your vagina will be tight enough to satisfy any man'. (Fine and Asch, 1988: 21). Greengross seems to endorse the notion that the sexual needs of disabled women are either nonexistent or inferior by writing, 'there is no doubt that women suffer the same pains of loneliness as men; and their sexual needs, though usually not as great, certainly exist' (Greengross, 1976: 110). Such an approach seriously undermines the sexuality of disabled women. There is no evidence to suggest that the sexual needs of women are any less than those of men (Coveney, *et al.*, 1984).

The reality for many disabled women is that the lack of social and employment opportunities may exacerbate the difficulties of establishing and maintaining relationships, particularly if a woman is living in her parental home.

> Personal relationships can be difficult if you live with your parents . . .
> The situation can be frustrating if you are at the age, as I am, when you
> could be living independently, working and travelling. Parents can be
> over-protective. (Campling, 1981: 17)

Given that many parents find it hard to come to terms with the fact that their children are sexual beings, it is not surprising that, where the daughter has a disability, parents find it particularly difficult to accept their child's sexuality. If a daughter appears to have a 'damaged' body or mind then parents might not be able to see why anybody else would be attracted to her. Consequently, they often convey negative attitudes to their disabled daughter and try to discourage any sexual development (See Rousso, 1978; Greengross, 1976; Campling, 1981: 80).

As an adolescent I realised that boys do not react in the same way to a girl in a wheelchair as they do to other girls . . . My mother did not help me during this, telling me to look for spiritual relationships because any man who appeared to be attracted to me must be perverted.

Sometimes men might be attracted to disabled women because they perceive disabled women as passive and more likely to respond to their sexual advances. Men who are threatened or intimidated by women who define their own sexual needs or appear as equals in a relationship may choose to focus their attentions on those women who seem to be in a less powerful position. Thus, men might choose to assert their power by establishing relations with the least powerful sections of the community such as disabled women, black women or single mothers.

Disabled women can challenge orthodox notions of the way people are expected to gain sexual satisfaction. For example, the traditional missionary position adopted in heterosexual relations may be totally inappropriate for many disabled women (as well as nondisabled women). Kirsten Hearn writes:

Different women with different disabilities have different needs and abilities, before, during and after sex. Some of us can only lie in certain positions or may have to use different parts of our bodies. Some of us have more strength and energy than others. (McEwen and O'Sullivan, 1988: 50)

The diverse range of methods used to gain sexual satisfaction by disabled women must be seen as a positive step for all women as it enables us to decide how our sexual needs can be met most sensitively.

There are sometimes distinct rules relating to the type of men that disabled women are allowed to have a relationship with or marry:

The invalid may marry another of his kind, and live happily or unhappily ever after. Society doesn't greatly care whether he is happy or unhappy as long as society isn't troubled. A wall is raised between the 'normal' world and the disabled – a wall 'invisible and hard and cold as unbreakable glass'. (Judith Thunem in Shearer, 1981: 84).

Greengross argues:

The principle problem for a marriage between an able-bodied person and someone handicapped is one of motivation. It begs the cruel and unavoidable question: 'What normal person would saddle him/herself with someone who probably will need a lifetime of care. Many 'normal' people when they enter a marriage of this nature are not marrying an equal but someone they want to treat like a child. (1976: 29)

This type of attitude is not only patronizing but also very insulting. It wrongly assumes that a disabled woman is passive, helpless and a burden. The persistent undermining of disabled women in such a way means that if we have a relationship with a nondisabled person then we are constantly subjected to the negative responses of other people:

> I am told how wonderful he is, and how lucky I am. It's great for the self-esteem . . . Implicit implication; he's wonderful/a saint for staying with an undesirable like you. You (disabled) are lucky not to be alone, unwanted in an institution. No one has ever said he is lucky (unthinkable), or he obviously stays with you because you give as much as you take. But then of course, that's an unthinkable proposition, isn't it? After all I'm only one of THE DISABLED. (Campling, 1981: 50)

Fine and Asch (1988) argue that the fact men want women who are not only visually attractive, but also functional in their role as a homemaker and wife means that disabled women are perceived as being incapable of fulfilling such a role.

Although society is organized and structured around heterosexual relationships, it must not be assumed that all disabled women are striving for marriage and motherhood. There are disabled women who have chosen to reject heterosexual relations and some of them will make a positive decision to be lesbian mothers. However, their experiences as lesbians can be extremely isolating.

> There's nobody here I can talk to really. I'm not telling the social worker or anyone at the centre. I'd get ostracised . . . I did tell someone years ago . . . He told me I could get treatment for it. I don't want that, I don't want my brain interfered with, there's enough wrong with me without that. (Gemma, 1989)

> When I came to live with my lesbian mate I felt a bit absurd about being gay and disabled . . . With her I was at ease of course, but I felt self-conscious about meeting other lesbians, I thought they'd see me as non-sexual, they'd think 'how can she be gay like us'. When I was passing for heterosexual it didn't occur to me to think I'd be regarded as non-sexual – I think this is because I saw heterosexual women as sexually passive anyway, whereas I see lesbians as equals. (Campling, 1981: 86)

> Severely able-bodied lesbians look at us and go, 'Urgh, what's *wrong* with her?' (McEwen and O'Sullivan, 1988: 50)

Some disabled lesbians argue that the lesbian community has adopted many of the values and expectations of the heterosexual community. Kirsten Hearn writes 'You only have to go to a disco to realize to what extent lesbians have bought the image of the slim, agile, symmetrical body' (McEwen and O'Sullivan, 1988: 50).

Both within the homosexual and heterosexual communities, disabled women have struggled to gain access to the same options as our nondisabled contemporaries. Unfortunately, our denied sexuality and exclusion from traditional gender roles has not exempted us from the threat or actuality of male sexual violence:

> Maria was twelve when her brother's closest friend began raping her regularly. He attacked her when she was in bed, unable to get to her wheelchair. He was eighteen, and powerful; she didn't stand a chance. (Matthews, 1983: 72)

As disabled women we can be much more vulnerable to sexual abuse and victimization, particularly if we have been bombarded with ideas that our bodies are a neutered object which is repulsive and inferior. A failure to recognize sexual development leaves us open to exploitation:

> A young woman of 14 who had a disability was raped by her teacher. He had fondled her and had intercourse with her. Because she had no sex education or values clarification, she didn't know that she didn't have to submit to this, and so she just went along. That is rape. That is coercion. As women we are taught to be passive. But if you are disabled very early on or when you are born, then this passivity is enculturated into what it means to be disabled and into the role of the disabled person. (Bogle, *et. al.,* 1951: 102)

> My first sexual experience was coercion, but I figured that nobody was even going to do it with me again, so I'd better get it now. I now feel that was rape. (Bogle, *et al.*, 1981: 102)

The perception that a disabled woman may never have sexual relations has been used as a justification for rape. One rapist said, 'I wanted to give her something that nobody else wanted to give' (Bogle, *et al.*, 1981: 102).

Disability Rag (1986) and Galler (1984) report instances where women with cerebal palsy have been ignored when they have reported rape. The effects of sexual violence can cause serious psychological and social problems for all women. However, as disabled women the problems we encounter can be magnified if we are perceived as asexual and not believed when we report rape. It is harder for us to leave exploitative or abusive relationships when we are trapped by our physical and financial dependence.

As disabled women, we are prescribed a life of passive dependence. Our neutered sexuality, negative body-image and restricted gender roles are a direct consequence of the processes and procedures which shape the lives of women.

Conclusion

When talking about disabled women, we are talking about women who have the same hopes, differences, anxieties, fears and other emotions as nondisabled women. The oppression we experience is similar to that encountered by our nondisabled sisters, but certain aspects are magnified in our daily lives, and others are altered to fit into the position that we hold as disabled people in society. There can be no doubt that for disabled women 'it is not difference which immobilizes us, but silence. And there are many silences to be broken' (Lorde, 1980: 15).

By applying the feminist principle of 'the personal is political', I have shown how disabled women have become misplaced and tolerated in a society which is both sexist and handicapist. Certain aspects of feminist analysis, particularly the concepts of gender roles, self-image, sexuality and socialization, have been used to highlight our experiences. Through such an analysis it has been possible to demonstrate how the concerns, needs, wishes and aspirations of disabled women strike at the core of the feminist movement, yet our voices usually remain unheard.

The feminist movement has restricted its thinking to the needs of nondisabled women. It has had difficulty tackling diversity among women, consequently many women, particularly those of us who have disabilities, have been left out in the cold. Feminism urgently needs to address the issue of diversity and in the process of doing this it must learn from the experiences of disabled women. It is crucial that 'the personal is political' is not simply used to provide an analysis of the experiences of a select group of women, namely white, nondisabled, heterosexual women, and that it goes beyond understanding immediate experiences to incorporate the needs and wishes of a diverse group of women. Charlotte Bunch explains, 'We cannot depend on our perceptions alone as the basis for political analysis and action – much less coalition. Feminists must stretch beyond, challenging the limits of our own personal experiences by learning from the diversity of women's lives (quoted in McEwen and O'Sullivan, 1988: 290).

In this article I have tried to break some of the silences surrounding the experiences of disabled women. Now the feminist movement needs to engage in an open dialogue with disabled women to learn from our experiences and develop a movement which reflects the diversity of the sisterhood. It is crucial that nondisabled feminists acknowledge our experiences and recognize our needs, wishes and aspirations as being a fundamental part of feminist experience and a key component of the feminist movement.

Writing from the perspective of a disabled woman, I can only conclude by emphasizing that the feminist movement has to accept the fact that disabled women have a right to full and equal participation. However, 'by this we don't mean just pity or embarrassment, or just plain access as outlined by us in the past, but an acceptance that we are viable, lovable and totally worthy members of the sisterhood'. (Kirsten Hearn quoted in McEwen and O'Sullivan, 1988: 53).

Notes

Nasa Begum is currently researching the needs and wishes of Asian people with disabilities. Before this she worked as a policy adviser in a local government women's unit. She continues to be actively involved in the disability rights, women's and race field in a personal and professional capacity.

References

BARRETT, M. and MCINTOSH, M. (1982) *The Anti-Social Family* London: Verso.

BECKER, E. F. (1978) *Female Sexuality after Spinal Cord Injury* Illinois: Accent Special Publications.

BEGUM, N. (1990) *The Burden of Gratitude* University of Warwick and SCA (Educational).

BOGLE, J. et al. (1981) 'Women's issues: a panel discussion' in BULLARD and KNIGHT.

BOSTON WOMEN'S HEALTH BOOK COLLECTIVE (1984) *The New Our Bodies Ourselves* New York: Simon & Schuster.

BROWNE, S. et al. (1985) editors, *With the Power of Each Breath* San Francisco: Cleis Press.

BULLARD, D. and KNIGHT, S (1981) editors, *Sexuality and Physical Disability* St Louis: C.V. Mosby Co.

CAMPLING, J. (1981) editor, *Images of Ourselves* London: Routledge & Kegan Paul

CARRILLO, A. et al. (1982) *No More Stares* Berkeley: Disability Rights Educational Defences Fund Inc.

COOK, L and ROSSETT, A. (1975) 'The sex role attitudes of deaf adolescent women and their implications for vocational choice' *American Annals of the Deaf* Vol. 20: 341–5.

COOTE, A. and CAMPBELL, B (1987) *Sweet Freedom* Oxford: Basil Blackwell.

COVENEY, L. et al. (1984) *The Sexuality Papers* London: Hutchinson.

CREEK, M. et al. (1987) *Personal and Social Implications of Spinal Cord Injury* Eltham: Thames Polytechnic.

DEEGAN, A and BROOKS, N (1985) editors, *Women and Disability: The Double Handicap* New Brunswick: Transaction Books.

DISABILITY RAG (1986) 'Care that Kills', *Disability Rag*, Vol. 7, No. 6: 9–10.

DUFFY, L. Y. (1981) in . . . All things are possible, M. I., A. J. Garvin and Associates.

FINCH, J. and GROVES, D. (1988) editors, *Caring: a Labour of Love*. London: Routledge & Kegan Paul.

FINE, M. and ASCH, A (1985) 'Disabled women: sexism without the pedestal' in DEEGAN and BROOKS.

—— (1988) editors, *Women with Disabilities – Essays in Psychology, Culture and Politics* Philadelphia: Temple University Press.

FINKEL et al. (1981) 'Sexuality and attendant care: a panel discussion' in BULLARD and KNIGHT

FISHER, S. (1973) *Body Consciousness* Englewood Cliffs: Prentice Hall.

FOX, G. (1980) 'The mother–adolescent daughter relationship as a sexual socialization structure: A research review' *Family Relations* Vol. 29: 21–8.

FRIEDMAN, G. (1980) 'The Mother–Daughter Bond' *Contemporary Psychoanalysis* Vol. 16, No. 1: 90–7.

GALLER, R. (1984) 'The myth of the perfect body' in VANCE.

GRAHAM, H. (1983) 'Caring: A labour of love, in FINCH and GROVES.

GEMMA (1979) *Newsletter No 7.*

—— (1989) *What's the Use of her Coming, She Can't Dance* London: Gemma.

GREENGROSS, W. (1976) *Entitled to Love* Guildford: National Marriage Guidance Council, in association with the National Fund for Research into Crippling Diseases.

GROTHAUS, R. (1985) 'Abuse of women with disabilities' in BROWNE et al. (1985).

HANNAFORD, S. (1985) *Living Outside Inside* Berkeley: Canterbury Press.

LANCASTER-GAYE, D. (1972) editor, *Personal Relationships, the Handicapped and the Community* London: Routledge & Kegan Paul.

LANDIS, C and BOLLES, M (1942) *Personality and Sexuality of the Physically Handicapped Woman* New York: Hoeber.

LORDE, A (1985) *The Cancer Journals* London: Sheba Feminist Publishers.

MATTHEWS, G. (1983) *Voices from the Shadows – Women with Disabilities Speak Out* Toronto: The Women's Press.

MCEWEN, C. and O'SULLIVAN, S. (1988) *Out the Other Side: Lesbian Contemporary Writing* London: Virago.

MORGAN, M. (1972) 'Attitudes of society towards sex and the handicapped' in LANCASTER-GAYE.

MORRIS, J. (1989) editor, *Able Lives* London: The Women's Press.

ROMANO, M. (1978) 'Sexuality and the disabled female' *Sexuality and Disability* Vol. 1, No. 1: 27–33.

ROUSSO, H. (1978) 'Daughters with disabilities: defective women or minority women? in FINE and ASCH (1988).

SHARPE, S. (1976) *Just Like a Girl* Harmondsworth: Penguin.

SHEARER, A (1981) *Disability Whose Handicap* Oxford: Basil Blackwell.

SMART, C. and SMART, B. (1976) *Women, Sexuality and Social Control* London: Routledge & Kegan Paul.

SUTHERLAND, A. (1981) *Disabled We Stand* London: Souvenir Press.

UNION OF PHYSICALLY IMPAIRED AGAINST SOCIETY (UPIAS) (1981) *Editorial from Disability Challenge* No. 1, May 1981.

VANCE, C (1984) *Pleasure and Danger* London: Routledge & Kegan Paul.

POSTCARD FROM THE EDGE: Thoughts on the 'Feminist Theory: An International Debate' Conference held at Glasgow University, Scotland, 12–15 July 1991

Susannah Radstone

> For if Ariadne has fled from the labyrinth of old, the only guiding thread
> for all of us now is a tightrope stretched above the void. (Braidotti,
> 1991: 15)

At the 'Feminist Theory' conference I met a woman who had arrived in
Britain with an Australian touring circus, and she told me a little of her
story. She said that she'd abandoned the world of the academy some
years ago for a life of physical adventure, but now, considering a return
to more intellectual pursuits, here she was at Glasgow, taking a look
around. Locked into conference mode, I faltered – what to talk about, if
not our institutions and the ups and downs of academic life? 'So, do you
walk the tightrope, or ride the trapeze?' I hazarded, eventually. 'No,
never, because it *hurts*!', was her emphatic and down-to-earth response.
Memories are notoriously slippery; partial, fractured, idiosyncratic and
screening, perhaps, as much as they reveal, but as I think back over
Glasgow, it's this fragment of a conversation – this glimpse of the circus
with its pains and its pleasures, that I recall.

'Feminist Theory: An International Debate' was a large event
although, with three hundred participants, sixty of them speakers,
attendance nevertheless fell two hundred short of the five hundred
women and sixty men who, so I've read, arrived in Oxford twenty-one
years ago for the first national gathering of the Women's Liberation
movement at Ruskin College.[1] Twenty-one years is a long time, and it's
tempting to draw comparisons between the two events – more tempting
still, perhaps, to construe the passing of those twenty-one years as
feminist theory's 'coming of age'. But that's a temptation best avoided,

for feminism's history stretches back a good deal further than a mere twenty-one years. To speak of feminism's coming of age would also place the many feminisms of Glasgow within one history and, by analogy, a normative one at that – the history of the individual's accession to 'equal rights'. More seriously still, perhaps, a 'coming of age' story implies, too, a degree of closure, whereas it's my hope that twenty-one years on, we're still only just beginning.

Ruskin and Glasgow were certainly very different events. To begin with, what Glasgow appeared to put on display was the extent of feminism's recent professionalization. Indeed, it sometimes seems as though feminism's arrival within the academy has coincided with the demise of that once powerful network of grass-roots organizations which, certainly in the seventies and early eighties, constituted the heart of the women's movement. The 1991 annual conference of the Women's Studies Network (UK) took place on the weekend prior to the Glasgow conference.[2] Here, representatives from women's pressure groups did speak alongside a truly international group of feminist academics, but so often, now, these groups appear to represent the interests of women *within* the academy, and to risk losing a more broad-based constituency outside educational establishments. At Glasgow, the conference participants – mainly white and middle class – were drawn, in the main, from those of us whose feminism is inextricably bound up with our professional lives within the academy. Unlike the Ruskin meeting, which was arguably an event *of* the women's movement, it is therefore as a predominantly academic-institutional event, at which feminist academics 'did theory', that Glasgow might most appropriately be remembered.

But how far did this difference of address and constituency shape the different agendas of Ruskin and Glasgow? Compared with Glasgow's super-abundance of plenaries and panels – with strands on 'psychoanalysis and the spectator' vying with those on 'gay identities' or 'representation and memory' in the first time-slot alone, the Ruskin College agenda appears stark in the extreme: 'the social role of women', 'women and the economy', 'women and revolution' and a final plenary which asked, simply, 'where are we going?'. Yet when I read about the Ruskin event, what's striking are the feelings of excitement, optimism and *shared* hope that it engendered, and when I remember Glasgow, it's with ambivalence. For me, it seems, Glasgow brought home the losses, as well as, or perhaps more than, the gains of the last twenty-one years. In my own paper for Glasgow, I discussed women's 'fictions of remembering' and argued, following Mary Jacobus (Jacobus: 1987), that although the suffusion of much feminist theory by nostalgia warrants careful critique, nostalgia nevertheless symptomatically evidences a wish – a wish that things could be different. Why, though, did Glasgow seem to me to evidence the loss of that previous moment's collective energy and hope? And how might we most productively learn from Glasgow's version of the current state of feminist theory?

The Glasgow event was neither divisive nor unhappy. From the 'wining and finger buffeting' of the opening Friday night reception, through the Sunday night social at the Glasgow Winter Gardens – with its vaulted glass roof, earthen floor, lights and music putting me in mind, once again, of the circus, to the closing plenary's pre-selected cross section of speakers, the show rolled smoothly. Twenty-one years on, feminist theory's relations with the newspapers, TV and radio appeared solid, if not entirely unproblematic, as a veritable media circus documented our activities from morning until night. An early morning radio encounter between one of the conference's organizers, Sandra Kemp, and the Conservative MP Edwina Currie, was followed by the arrival of the *Daily Telegraph*'s photographers, who were, strangely, and much to the dismay of the majority of women participants, ejected from the main conference hall due to the loud objections of one male participant, and who were later to be seen taking snapshots of the conference organizers on the steps of the main venue. By any of the 'performance indicators' of academic enterprise, then, Glasgow was undoubtedly a success. Uncoincidentally, perhaps, it is around this concept of performance that many of the questions prompted for me by Glasgow have come to settle.

My first, and perhaps keenest intimation of unease came on Friday night, when, at the opening reception, held in the awesome marbled halls of the Kelvingrove Art Gallery, Glasgow's Lord Provost – a woman – delivered a heart-rending speech of welcome. She felt, she told us all, an abiding sense of gratitude for and commitment to the struggles which had enshrined women's – and especially working-class women's – rights to education, since, as a child of the Glasgow tenements, it was via education that she had accomplished her undoubtedly tough journey from the Gorbals to the civic hall. This was a story that moved me, a story told bravely, and a story told from the heart – a story, though, which appeared destined to fall into the void. For, unlike at Ruskin, at Glasgow there remained no place, apparently, for the questions implicitly raised by the Lord Provost's welcoming address – questions about women and class, women and education, and women and the welfare state, to name but a few. In the all-too-brief closing question-time, one participant argued that this absence should be seen as the absence of the sociologists from Glasgow. But although there were, indeed, few sociologists at the conference, my own view is that we are all, in each of our disciplines, equally responsible for the difficulties in which feminist theory – from its inception, always an interdisciplinary area – now finds itself. It would therefore be inappropriate to demand of the sociologists alone a reconstructed theory that can resituate these questions on feminism's agenda.

In response to the criticism that the conference lacked so-called 'sociological' debate, Kemp explained that, although the original call for papers had invited such contributions, 90 per cent of the abstracts received concerned themselves entirely with questions of subjectivity. This state of affairs was clearly overdetermined. In part, the conference's focus on subjectivity must surely have been due to the networks and grapevines extending from Glasgow University's English department – home to the conference administration, as well as to Sandra Kemp. The arguably growing rift between feminist theory within the academy and feminist practice on the 'outside' must also have played some part in shaping Glasgow's agenda. But like a small boat struggling, if not adrift in the storm, Glasgow's agenda most certainly evidenced, perhaps above all, what Rosa Braidotti referred to recently as 'the ontological insecurity we suffer [as] our unavoidable historical condition' (Braidotti: 1991: 2). With hindsight, and perhaps unfairly, one might have hoped for a second and more strategic call for papers in those over-determinedly absent areas. Glasgow, though, was clearly shaped, more than anything, by those insecurities and doubts which currently shake feminist theory to its core, producing a range of questions concerning the status of the category 'woman': is a politics grounded in women's *collective* experience still desirable, given poststructuralism's deconstruction of binary oppositions? Should we not acknowledge more fully differences between women, as well as differences which cut across the man/woman opposition? Can 'woman' be thought outside of biological essentialism, and if so, how? Given this agenda, the question I want to ask – and it's a vexing one – is this: can the 'ontological insecurity' at the heart of feminist theory's engagements with poststructuralism and postmodernism be negotiated without consigning the voice of that woman from the Gorbals to the void? Or are such endeavours doomed to break up on the rocks of the essentialism/anti-essentialism debate?[3] And did Glasgow – or, more properly, the conference route that I as one participant took – seek or offer answers to these questions?

My second moment of unease came during the Saturday morning opening session of the 'conference proper', a performance by the V-girls – five women who tour a ninety-minute skit of a feminist literary conference, this time a conference about *Heidi*. The show had us in stitches. They lampooned Lacan and parodied the feminist literary theorist's love of repetition and alliteration. Keen evocations of the paradoxical imbrication of academic sisterhood with competitive institutional politics followed on the heels of a sharp attack on those tightrope walkers who embrace poststructuralism whilst insisting on the authority of their textual analyses – an attack to which several later speakers self-mockingly (and defensively) returned. The V-girls performed feminists performing feminist theory and we laughed. But their act, and the world it represented was so very bleak and cold.[4] And at the heart of this performance there lay a desire – a (nostalgic?) desire for less ambivalent modes of female bonding.

For some though, perhaps, the V-girls' performance of performance might have appeared consonant with the French theorist Luce Irigaray's championing of the subversive performance, or mimicry of 'the feminine', a practice she terms *mimesis*. Without doubt, Irigaray was a central figure at Glasgow – this centrality due largely to the contested status of her work within the essentialism/anti-essentialism debates. Recently, the essentialist charge raised against her 'theory of sexual difference' has been parried less by attempts to reclaim her work for anti-essentialism than by attempts to move beyond what some now see as a debate pivoting round a disabling and reductive opposition.[5] One example of such work was Mary Orr's paper, 'Genesis, gynesis and ontogenesis', which took off from Irigaray and Weil to offer a theory of what she called 'ontogeny' by which she meant a theory of woman's being and becoming, as a route through and beyond essentialism. But although Orr claimed to have moved beyond essentialism, her very abstract theory did not seem to me to offer us a way of 'thinking women' in all our many and varied differences from each other, and so threatened to consign to the void once again that specific and concrete voice from the Gorbals.

One feminist theoretician whose work has most frequently been aligned with anti-essentialism is Teresa de Lauretis. (see, for example, Schor: 1989). Most recently, however, de Lauretis's most visible undertaking has been that of bringing to light the work of the Italian feminist group known as the Milan Women's Bookstore Collective – a group for whom, as de Lauretis points out in her introduction to their book *Sexual Difference: A Theory of Social-Symbolic Practice* (reviewed elsewhere in this volume) – Irigaray's influence has been formative. De Lauretis's championing of the Milan Women's Bookstore Collective's work must be viewed in the context of her recent advocacy of 'taking the risk of essentialism seriously', (de Lauretis: 1989) since now, her key concern is to distinguish not between essentialism and nonessentialism, but between two understandings of essentialism: on the one hand, essence understood as the 'thing-in-itself' and on the other hand essence understood as the properties, qualities and necessary attributes to which women have historically been bound. (de Lauretis: 1989: 5)

To some degree, like de Lauretis, the Glasgow conference, too, sought to bring the work of the Milan Women's Bookstore Collective, as well as that of other Italian feminist groups, to greater international prominence. At the 'Women's Studies Network (UK)' conference, indeed, Rosa Braidotti joked that the Glasgow programme looked more than anything like a marketing job for Italian feminism. At least sixty Italian participants, including several speakers, came to Glasgow, and a team of diligent translators were constantly on hand to further international understanding.

At the heart of the Milan Women's Bookstore Collective's work lies the practice of *affidamento* (entrustment): a relationship in which one women entrusts herself, symbolically, to another woman, while acknowledging disparities of class, age, status, and so on. Central, too, to their work is the concept of *la madre simbolica* (the symbolic mother), a figure that represents a *female* value and which enables *affidamento*. It is this *female* value which grounds *affidamento*, since it represents a 'plus' which exists outside of patriarchal divisions of status, class, and so on. In her introduction to their collected papers, de Lauretis proposes that *Sexual Difference*'s understanding of the difference of woman should best be seen not as a difference that takes off from biology, but as 'a difference of symbolisation, a different production of reference and meaning out of a particular embodied knowledge' (Milan Women's Bookstore Collective: 1990: 13). One hope at Glasgow must surely have been that the Italian feminism of *Sexual Difference*, as interpreted by de Lauretis, might offer one path through the impasse of the essentialism/anti-essentialism debates. But, as de Lauretis herself acknowledges, 'this theory of female social-symbolic practice makes little space for differences and divisions between – and especially within – women, and so tends to construct a view of the female social subject that is too clearly modelled on the "monstrous subject" of philosophy and History.' (Milan Women's Bookstore Collective: 1991: 18). From this perspective, then, that voice from the Gorbals – a voice that is at once female, working class, urban and Scottish, threatens, once more, to fall into the void.

A further question raised by the presence of the Italian feminists – by no means all of them followers of the Milan Women's Bookstore Collective – at Glasgow, concerns the cross-national 'translatability' of situated and strategically nuanced feminist theories. Although Glasgow's profile as 'international debate' implicitly raised this question, the sessions I attended omitted to extend debate in that important area. Barbara Godard's paper 'Feminist fictions of transformation', did, however, concern itself with the act of *literary* translation – that of translating the Quebecoise feminist writer Nicole Brossard's *Picture Theory* into English, and, in so doing, performed another now rather well – if not overrehearsed feminist strategy for negotiating our current 'ontological insecurity': the situating of feminist theoretical work within autobiographical writing. Godard's journal excerpts cited Jacques Derrida, among many poststructuralists and deconstructivists, to tell the story of translation as one of intertextuality, and sought thereby to underline the contingent status of all translation. But in her insistent listing of all her textual influences, as well as her moods and life-events during the project, the tightrope she walked appeared to risk substituting the translator's subjectivity for the text's authority.

Autobiographical 'snippets' appeared almost *de rigeur* at Glasgow, where the now hackneyed opening gambit of 'as I sat at my word-processor the other night wondering about what to write for my conference paper' was endlessly repeated. But although such self-referential comments now feature as *the* clichés of feminist theoretical work, not every deployment of autobiography at Glasgow was so predictable. Following Godard, a second autobiographical performance came from Nancy Miller, whose paper, 'Getting personal' produced a clearly subjective and situated voice to knowingly and strategically undermine her authority as white, middle-class, East Coast, heterosexual, high-status feminist. This paper, which combined personal reminiscence with public life-history, constituted a nostalgic retrospective of the development of US academic feminism – and regretfully acknowledged lost opportunities for the establishment of wider and deeper alliances between women in the academy and a broad range of diversely situated women 'on the outside'. To my mind, it was the fractured yet coherent voice of this paper which I found most moving, for its power and its agility – its successful negotiation of a tightrope – lay in its undercutting of the well-rehearsed, accomplished and supremely confident voice of the public university professor, with the hesitant, troubled and yet committed voice of the private woman. But perhaps, as one participant suggested, this strategy's capacity to undermine certain forms of feminist authority depends, paradoxically, upon their conservation: for the 'bite' of personal revelation can depend, like tabloid journalism, upon the fame of its subject.

In a single report, there's space only to touch on those aspects of a conference of this size that appeared significant through the prism of my own theoretical concerns. No space here, then, to do more than mention the staged confrontation between two attempts to formulate a new feminist materialism, those of Rosa Braidotti's Foucauldian-Deleuzian politics of embodiment, versus Elizabeth Grosz's Derridian-Benvenistean quest for corporeal traces and sexual signatures. No space to do more than gesture towards the influential position Glasgow accorded to Judith Butler's *Gender Trouble* (Butler, 1990), or to document the critiques offered of her politics of parody. No space here to do more than note that while for Butler, lesbian and gay camp and drag are acknowledged as her inspiration, the seeming centrality of lesbianism for the Milan Women's Bookstore Collective, is, as de Lauretis explains, hotly disputed. (Milan Women's Bookstore Collective, 1991: 15–19) And, sadly, no space to ponder lesbianism's *quiet* presence at this conference.

Across the midnight blue cover of *Patterns of Dissonance* (Braidotti: 1991), stretches a tightrope, and on this tightrope, arms outstretched, is poised a tiptoed figure whose status as embodied being or mechanical figure remains ambiguous: a fitting image indeed with which to represent feminist theory's current precariousness. I'll choose to end this report by celebrating one Glasgow performance which walked this tightrope and had me, for one, holding my breath. Ailbhe Smyth's paper, 'A reading from the book of beginnings' was performed twice: first, in the panel entitled 'postmodernism', and then, fittingly – given the term's critical status within theories of femininity – as an *encore* with which to close the final plenary. Smyth's 'a reading . . .' tiptoed across more than one tightrope: part poetry, part theory, she told her own story, her own life, by means of quotation, and by means of Irish folktale and riddle, thereby posing a series of questions about narrative, about autobiography, about performance and about the status of theories such as those of postmodernism within our lives and work. In a recent issue of *Differences*, Wendy Brown comments that feminist theory's recently acquired skills in 'politicising the "I"' may be 'at odds with the requisites for developing a political conversation among a complex and diverse "we".' (Brown: 1991). Perhaps one strategy for negotiating this tightrope was offered by one participant – Maureen McNeil's – response to Smyth's presentation, for as she put it, what we risk, in our autobiographical work is a fall into narcissism, but what we gain, when it works, is a discourse that 'pushes out'. For me, Smyth's paper did precisely that, it 'pushed out', engaging and moving me by enacting what Gayatri Chakravorty Spivak has described recently as 'a sort of deconstructive homeopathy, a deconstructing *of* identities by identities . . . by thinking of oneself as an example of certain kinds of . . . narratives. A . . . claiming of an identity from a text that comes from somewhere else.' (Spivak: 1989) Perhaps here, at least, we find the beginnings of a practice that can rescue the voice from the Gorbals from the void. A tightrope walked, then, to end the conference: a conference at which the woman from the circus may have felt more at home than she expected?

Notes

Susannah Radstone teaches English, Film and Cultural Studies at Keele University. She's the editor of *Sweet Dreams: Sexuality, Gender and Popular Fiction* and assistant editor of *The Women's Companion to International Film.* She's currently writing a book on women's film and fiction 1970–90 to be published by Routledge.

1 The Ruskin Women's Weekend was the first national meeting of the Women's Liberation movement. It was held on the weekend of Friday 27 February–Sunday 1 March 1970. For one woman's brief retrospective account of this event, see Condon (1990: 25–8), and also the memories of contributors to Wandor (1990).
2 'New Directions For Women's Studies in the 1990s', the 1991 conference of the Women's Studies Network (UK) was co-ordinated by Hilary Hinds and Jackie Stacey. It took place at Camden School for Girls, London, on the weekend of 6–7 July.
3 For an extremely comprehensive and stimulating overview of the current state of play in this debate see the special issue of *Differences* (1989).
4 For a brief, critical review of the V-girls in performance, see Light (1990).
5 Irigaray's work has been the subject of several recent anglophone reinterpretations. For the most recent of these see Whitford: 1991. For an anti-essentialist reading of her work, see Schor: 1989.

References

BRAIDOTTI, Rosa (1991) *Patterns of Dissonance: A Study of Women in Contemporary Philosophy* Cambridge: Polity Press.
BROWN, Wendy (1991), 'Feminist hesitations, postmodern exposures' in *Differences* Vol. 3, No. 1, Spring.
BUTLER, Judith (1990) *Gender Trouble: Feminism and the Subversion of Identity* New York and London: Routledge.
CONDON, Judith (1990) 'The women's weekend: the beginning of a movement' in *Women: A Cultural Review* Vol. 1, No. 1, April: 25–8.
DE LAURETIS, Teresa (1989) 'The essence of the triangle or taking the risk of essentialism seriously: feminist theory in Italy, the US and Britain' in *Differences* (1989).

DIFFERENCES (1989) Special issue on 'Essentialism' Vol. 1, No. 2, Summer.

JACOBUS, Mary (1987) 'Freud's mnemonic: women's screen memories and feminist nostalgia' in *Michegan Quarterly Review* No. 1, Fall.

LIGHT, Alison (1990) 'Theoretical "V" signs' in *Artscribe* September/October.

MILAN WOMEN'S BOOKSTORE COLLECTIVE (1990) *Sexual Difference: A Theory of Social-Symbolic Practice* Bloomington: Indiana University Press.

SCHOR, Naomi (1989) 'This essentialism which is not one: coming to grips with Irigaray' in *Differences* (1989).

SPIVAK, Gayatri Chakravorty, (1989) '"In a word": Gayatri Chakravorty Spivak in conversation with Ellen Rooney' in *Differences* (1989).

WANDOR, Michelene (1990) editor, *Once A Feminist: Stories of A Generation* London: Virago.

WHITFORD, Margaret (1991) *Luce Irigaray: Philosophy in the Feminine* London: Routledge.

REVIEW ESSAY

Sally Munt

Lesbian Texts and Contexts: Radical Revisions
edited by Karla Jay and Joanne Glasgow
Onlywomen Press: London 1992 ISBN 0906500 40 0 £8.95 Pbk

Lesbian and Gay Writing
edited by Mark Lilly, Macmillan Press: Basingstoke, 1990.
ISBN 9 780333 475 010 £9.99 Pbk

The Safe Sea of Women: Lesbian Fiction 1969–1989
Bonnie Zimmerman, Onlywomen Press: London 1992
ISBN 0906500 42 7 £7.95 Pbk

Teaching courses in lesbian culture over the past five years, I've become
frustratedly aware of how proliferating but disparate and difficult to pin
down most of the critical material is. Tracking down the elusive pieces of
literary criticism is tantamount to lesbian detecting: articles appear
and disappear, and information on their whereabouts depends on
having friends in the know. There are signs, however, that the field is
cohering into a discrete discipline; 1990 produced two anthologies, the
imported *Lesbian Texts and Contexts: Radical Revisions*, edited by
Karla Jay and Joanne Glasgow, and homegrown British *Lesbian and
Gay Writing*, edited by Mark Lilly. Two recent bibliographic references,
Out On the Shelves, produced by British librarians in the wake of
Section 28, and New Zealander Miriam Saphira's *New Lesbian Literature 1980–88*, suggest there is also a fictional canon to collect.
    Galvanized in part by the repressive legislation of the 1980s (soon
to be followed by more of the same, no doubt), British and North
American lesbian and gay activism has provoked a self-reflective
growth in cultural theory. The new decade will see its maturity and
expansion – already two English universities have held conferences:
'The Future for Lesbian and Gay Studies' (Essex), and 'Questions of
Homosexuality' (London).
    However, it is appropriate that the first book-length genre study

should be written by Bonnie Zimmerman, whose article 'What has never been: an overview of lesbian feminist literary criticism', now ten years old, has stood, with Catherine Stimpson's 'Zero degree deviancy: the lesbian novel in English' (both 1981) as a reference point for much subsequent work. Each has also borne the overdetermined responsibility of being the token article straight academics may have heard of, and even quote from. Barbara Smith's article 'Towards a black feminist criticism' (1970) has also served this purpose.

Zimmerman's new book, *The Safe Sea of Women*, winner of a 1990 LAMBDA literary award, is an overview from an undetached critic; she writes 'not as an outsider looking in, but as an insider looking around' (xvii). It is her own felt relation to these texts which makes the book such an engaging read. Its ideal reader, 'a composite figure who is a feminist academic and a lesbian activist', is also part of this textual community; someone, like me, for whom the fiction has had personal, historical repercussions. By addressing such a reader, the text drew me in, in a way literary theory usually does not.

Lesbians share a highly literary subculture, certain novels are linchpins of individual and corporate lives; they are points of reference, (w)rites of passage. Zimmerman avoids universalizing clichés by self-consciously positioning herself as a critic with a specific culture and history. The integrity of the book results from the considered awareness which combines a scholarly, literary aesthetic with a lesbian-feminist consciousness. When examining these fictionalized 'myths of origins', she extrapolates from the texts a manifestation of the Lesbian Nation, a conceptual utopia and shared culture which so far has largely been the creation of white Western women. The image has a literary home in Monique Wittig's *The Lesbian Body* and *Lesbian Peoples*, but other legacies from gay life before Stonewall, 1960s counterculture, radical feminism, and intertextual literary symbols inform the vision. Zimmerman describes how lesbians tend to look back to an imaginary golden age 'when we lived free and proud in our own separate territory'. This desire locates itself in a metaphorical island, which is surrounded by a safe sea of women.

The author observes how lesbian community exists more happily in literature and myth than in real life, and she goes on to show how the romantic mecca must be splintered by difference. The exclusivity of Lesbos is challenged by a politics of diverse identities, to be replaced by a cosmopolitan archipelago – comprising Carriacou, Jamaica, Calafia, Aztlan, Moab and others. She writes:

> By avoiding difference the lesbian community becomes a microcosm of the dominant culture, and our transforming myths come back to haunt us. If we predicate 'sameness' and 'unity' upon the culture, values, and beliefs of only one group of women, and these women (no matter how self-defined as outlaws) belong to the dominant culture, Lesbian Nation becomes an imperialist nation.

Drawing from her analysis of texts from 1969–89, Zimmerman suggests that, on the whole, the fiction of the 1970s posited a universal lesbian type, or 'core identity', whereas the fiction of the 1980s began to disenfranchise this essentialism.[1] Taking on the poststructuralist resort to a fragmented self, she challenges this image's appropriateness, asking 'Is this holistic self nevertheless *necessary* to subjects who have been denied [a] unified identity?'. Using the concept of a *multivalent* self – one that permits combination, interaction and change – she extrapolates from Lorde's *Zami* an idea of selfhood which is neither essentialist nor nostalgic, but

> fluid, shimmering, and mobile, because it is a self whose 'place [is] the very house of difference rather than the security of any one particular difference'. (*Zami*: 226)

Lesbian fiction expresses four dimensions within a myth of origins: the lesbian self, the lesbian couple, the lesbian community, and community and difference. These divisions have been progressive and developmental – although latterly, Zimmerman notes, visions of the Lesbian Nation are weaker and more diffuse, as fiction becomes more individualistic and idiosyncratic. It is as though 'the center of Lesbian Nation no longer holds'. While the book ends on a note of reflective retreat, the author also contends that this movement of self-criticism is characteristic of lesbian culture, 'our fiction continually sets up a version of reality and then pulls it down again'. *The Safe Sea of Women* is not intended to be 'the' authoritative version of the genre of lesbian fiction, but it is the most distinctly articulate and expressive deciphering of the field.

Lesbian and Gay Writing has been published as one of the 'Insights' series, developing a range of resource books on contemporary cultural criticism. These anthologies are for the lay or busy reader who wants short, sharp bites of meaning rather than the slowly developmental satisfaction gained from a nine-course dinner, or monograph. Snacking tends to be vaguely unfulfilling however, thus this collection is not for those hungry for the definitive lesbian/gay critical hermeneutic. (It would be largely indigestible for those liberal left lecturers longing for the one-week lesbian/gay angle for inclusion on literary theory option courses.)

This book is impressionistically polyphonic, resisting the idea that lesbian/gay writing emanates from a single viewpoint. Conversely, this may also be perceived as a lack: there is no explanation as to why these discrete subcultures should have a common aesthetic. There are common themes however, supporting the impetus for a set of problematics around parody, displacing gender, hetero-critique, interrogation of identity and voice, and alienation. Against these innovative themes is set the conventional backdrop of Literature, coldly felt by those outside that cosy canon.

If I sound defensive, then perhaps the book's intended audience could be borne in mind, i.e., those academics and students wishing to embrace 'neglected literary and cultural areas' (series introduction). It is the purpose of reviews to concoct summary judgements of any given text, and in reviewing this book it is indeed this flavour of rehabilitation, of truth established, which provides its *raison d'être*. This self-justifying cautiousness of British criticism contrasts with the enterprising, celebratory, evangelistic tenor of its American counterpart.

In the half of the book shared by the lesbian contributors, with the exception of Caroline Halliday's essay on 'Contemporary lesbian erotic poetry', the emphasis is on historical material. Susan Crecy's short essay on Ivy Compton-Burnett, 'Family as nightmare', is a literary extrapolation of her covert lesbianism, her novels constitute 'one of the most far-reaching onslaughts in the history of literature on hetero-sexuality's most revered institution[s]'. This essay just falls short of replicating the stereotype of the embittered homosexual. Lyndie Brimstone's essay is a copious and comprehensive guide to Maureen Duffy's writing, not before time. Diane Hamer's piece on Ann Bannon's pulp romances of the 1950s is tightly argued and likely to win the prize for the 'chapter-most-likely-to-be-illegally-photocopied'. She argues that Bannon's refusal to settle on any definitive cause for lesbianism situates the reader in self-conscious exploration:

> Bannon's writing more often than not describes *positions* around which desire is organised, in which the roles themselves can be put on or taken off as easily as clothes.

This essay, by exploring desire and sexual identity as historical entities, rather endorses the view that when it comes to developing critiques of sexuality, we got there first.

Caroline Halliday's romp through erotic poetry is another copious overview, replete with queerly quixotic little quotes for those quietly quivering moments when lifting belly. My favourites were Marilyn Hacker's

> I almost came in my new herringbones
> in the Via degli Alfani, just
> imagining your socks off

and Halliday's own

> Pubic flesh crusts against yours small fat
> flesh creeps close to tangents that deny
> give way, cool burning lines dagger across
> me, slide into your small soft throated
> arsehole, touching lines of silver flesh.

Most poems revert to natural metaphors, myself I prefer the literal. In contrast to her own poem above, the article is paradoxically coy, often referring to the 'shock value' of the texts, and privileging romantic types of sex. The author asks whether lesbian poetry allows us to investigate difficult feelings; I wished she'd been more forthright within her own piece, but we return to the limitations inscribed in the book's intended audience.

Finally, Gillian Spraggs' 'Exiled to home: the poetry of Sylvia Townsend Warner and Valentine Ackland' is a little gem. Spraggs's style achieves the balance between descriptive narrative and interpretative criticism, leading the reader seductively into a sympathetic identification with Warner/Ackland's unacknowledged creative partnership. The 1982 edition of Warner's *Collected Poems* omitted any contribution from the volume *Whether a Dove or Seagull*, love poems from each woman to the other. Claire Harman's recent introduction to Warner's 1936 novel, *Summer Will Show*, reprinted by Virago in 1987, is equally reticent. This connects me in a neatly circumfluous fashion back to Mark Lilly's Introduction, an apologia for lesbian/gay writing which rests on its historical obscurity, and its concomitant and now necessary uncovering. I am reminded of the 'Dorset Scene' course I did as an undergraduate in Weymouth. Every Friday afternoon we would walk the landscape with our lecturer ebulliently extolling the landmarks of the literati. When passing the cottage shared by both lovers in East Chaldon, only Warner was mentioned. Valentine Ackland, a writer in her own right, was, like Warner's lesbianism, cast into literary incognita. It's a model for this volume's existence.

Lesbian Texts and Contexts: Radical Revisions took me weeks to read; with twenty-two original chapters running to nearly four hundred pages, and a hardback price of fifty-six dollars, I felt like a tentative *ingénue*, odyssey-bound. Onlywomen Press is publishing a much cheaper British edition. Increasingly, I became convinced that things are bigger and better Over There. The strengths of this volume owe a lot to the fact that Lesbian Studies started in North America in 1977 (according to Catherine Stimpson) and, having become relatively established during the 1980s, can now be both canonized and critiqued in the 1990s. A most delightful sense of diversity diffuses this collection: three parts, 'Writers and Their Work', 'Lesbian Encodings, Decodings', and 'Lesbian Themes, Sources', contain essentialist and social-constructionist approaches, realistic and experimental styles of writing, historical and contemporary contexts, and investigations of the author/text/reader as sites of intrigue.

An ensuing and insinuating aspect of these speculations caused this reader at least to interrogate that slippery term 'lesbian'. Indeed, as a critical category, 'lesbian' got more and more complex and circuitous as I read on. 'Is lesbianism a metaphor?', asks Catherine Stimpson,

> For 'lesbianism' might signify a critique of heterosexuality; a cry for the abolition of the binary oppositions of modern sexuality; a demand for the release of women's self-named desires; a demand that such release might itself be a sign of a rebellious, subtle, raucous textuality. 'Lesbianism' might represent a space in which we shape and reshape our psychosexual identities, in which we are metamorphic creatures.

Lesbian literary theory like this offers us the lesbian-as-sign, both as an absence (in the textual gaps and spaces into which a lesbian reading can slide, for example in Bonnie Zimmerman's essay on George Eliot), or a presence, as a radical signifier, rupturing the phallocentric subject (as Namascar Shaktini claims in her chapter on Monique Wittig's *The Lesbian Body*).

In engaging with contemporary theories such as 'deconstruction', lesbian literary theory can interface with the conceptual élite of Western criticism; without wishing to impugn this theoretical creativity, however, I want to express a (cavilling?) concern, i.e., what has all this got to do with us Naiad fans, drooling for generic romance number 42? Isn't this kind of uncritical consumption just a trifle *conventional* at times? Sometimes I want my reading to be the very opposite of an intellectual challenge. There still seems to be a dichotomy between theory and experience, and even theory and activism. Going on a Section 25 or 28 march, reading some pink pulp, and discoursing on the dialectic of deferred desire in Nicole Brossard do require different hats.

It now seems a given that a decade of identity politics has mobilized and positively affirmed lesbian lifestyle and culture as radically oppositional to dominant forms of gender and sexuality. Drawing this model over criticism suggests that lesbian writing, or literary theory, will *inevitably* undermine/disarm its target institution, Literature. Most of this new work is self-consciously aware of its pioneering status and is careful to problematize, rather than pronounce. Hence what interests me is these critics' engagement with questions like: how accurately can the term 'radical' be applied to lesbian textuality, how does this relate to lesbian identity, and how can this be distinct from any other oppositional, interpretative strategy? And there's more . . .

Notes

Sally Munt is a Lecturer in the Humanities Department at Brighton Polytechnic. She is currently working on a Ph.D. on genre and feminist fiction, and has edited a collection, *New Lesbian Criticism: Literary and Cultural Readings* Spring 1992, Harvester Wheatsheaf.

1 Recently Diana Fuss (1990) has argued that essentialist types of identity are responses by subcultures to external oppression, in which case, if the fiction of the 1980s has in part rejected these structures, it may suggest a feeling of greater freedom, in conflict with the prevailing consensus regarding the decade's political disillusionment.

References

FUSS, Diana (1990) *Essentially Speaking* London: Routledge.
LORDE, Audre (1982) *Zami* London: Sheba Feminist Publishers.

REVIEWS

Armed Angels: Women in Iran

Mandana Hendessi

CHANGE, (International Reports, No. 16): London, 1990 £2.30 Pbk

Armed Angels: Women in Iran is a detailed historical analysis of women's position in Iranian society from 1850–1990.

Mandana looks at women's position in three separate and yet related periods. First, she examines the deep-rooted patriarchal relations in Iranian society between 1850 to the beginning of the Pahlavi dynasty, 1926. She argues that, prior to Islam, the male-dominated nature of society ensured that women exercised little control over their lives. She suggests that Iranian women's oppression, and consequently their veiling, was largely due to prevailing social conditions rather than the moral teachings of the Koran.

Focusing on the period between 1926–1978, under the Pahlavi regime, she looks at worldwide socio-economic changes and their impact on Iranian society, particularly issues concerning women's place in the family and workplace. The third section is devoted to an analysis of women's position within radical Islam generated by Shariati, as well as women's practical experiences under Khomeini and the post-Khomeini era.

The strength of her pamphlet is the way in which she attempts to provide comprehensive historical evidence of Iranian women's subordination, rather than the more narrow approach of looking at Islam as the main cause of women's oppression. However, we should not overlook the importance of the role played by Islam in perpetuating and strengthening women's subordination in all aspects of life, at all times. Furthermore, to suggest, as Mandana does, that 'women's seclusion was not ordained by Islam', is overly general and brief. To argue the case successfully, she needs to provide historical evidence about the conditions that led to women's oppression in the pre-Islamic period, and more detail about the specific forms that this oppression took. By looking at the period from 1850–1990, one cannot say anything about the pre-Islamic period.

Throughout, Mandana provides historical events to show how the unity between Islamic institutions and ruling bodies has always managed to ensure that women are kept under control. Also, she demonstrates how women's active participation in, and mobilization for, politics has been motivated in order to defend the 'nation', and to make it possible for them to perform their 'patriotic duty' without any political gains and rewards as women.

By looking at major events such as the Tobacco Crisis of 1891–92 and the constitutional revolution of 1905–11, she explains how increased Western penetration of Iranian society led to the development of Western Victorian models of life. Women's activity during the Tobacco Crisis, and their part in the constitutional revolution, was highly significant and impressive. Unfortunately, they fought for a constitution which stated that only men had the right to vote and be elected.

The Pahlavi era was one of rapid modernization and industrialization that affected the whole structure of society. Women were encouraged towards further education and a higher degree of public participation. The price of these gains, however, was paid for by women ruthlessly being forced to unveil and dress in accordance with state policies. To placate the *Ulama*, Reza Shah made sure that women were kept inferior by incorporating part of *shari'a* into the new body of Iranian civil law. Under this law, a man could divorce his wife when he pleased, while a woman could divorce only on specific grounds such as impotence and infidelity. Also, women's inheritance rights were less than those of men. The husband was constituted as the head of the family with legal control over the children. Most importantly, women were not able to vote or stand as candidates in election to the Mazlis (parliament).

The centralization of political power resulted in the rigid control of women's employment, education and clothing. The counterforce to these repressive measures took different forms. However, it was really only during the 1940s that women's political organizations, which had been suppressed for so long, began to emerge. Women's active participation during the nationalist insurgency, led by the Democratic organization of Iranian Women (DOIW), mobilized masses of veiled, as well as unveiled, women. Once again their demands around economic independence, state welfare for poor women and children, equality of men and women, review of the marriage law, wage equality, and maternity leave for all women workers (including domestic workers), took second place to the proposals of the nationalist leadership which included some of the *Ulama*.

The crushing of the nationalist movement by the Shah (backed by Britain and the United States), meant further suppression of all the opposition organizations. *Armed Angels* looks at the political, social and economic implications of the Shah's 'white revolution', and the effect of the quadrupling of oil prices on the lives of Iranian women.

Mandana's analysis of women's resistance and opposition contains certain weaknesses. Although the impact of socio-economic circumstances is discussed in detail, very little is said in a systematic way about the political and organizational forms of women's struggle during the ninety years of successive governments.

She refers to the existence of women's independent organizations which were crushed by 1930, but does not explain what this tradition was and which organizations she is referring to. A more complete picture of this would require a discussion of the aims and objectives of the forms of their resistance, their weaknesses and strengths. She could also have discussed what the aims and objectives of the following organizations were: The Society of Masked Women (Arjuman-i zanans Negabpush, 1911); Patriotic Women (Nesvan-i vatkanha, 1922); Messengers of Happiness (Pazk-i Saadat, 1922); Association of Women's Revolution (Mazma'eh Ingilabe Zanan, 1922); Awakening of Tehran Women (Bidari-yi Nesvan-i Tehran, 1926).

The lack of systematic analysis of the women's movement allows her to overlook the importance of the role that could have been played by the left, both before and during the 1979 revolution. She refers only to the left's ambiguous and unspecific position on the question of women.

Without looking in detail at women's theoretical and practical experiences, it is not possible to provide a precise account of the conditions which left them unarmed, isolated and easy targets to crush. Unfortunately, in most cases the left organizations either believed there was no 'women's question' at all, or their support for women's equality and emancipation was there mainly to recruit more women.

In the final section, Mandana looks at the conditions of women within radical Islam and under Khomeini's rule, and explains how the idea of armed angels became a revolutionary theory. Before going further, it is important to look at her definition of 'armed angels'. In the introduction she suggests the contradictory policy changes concerning women for the last ninety years: 'Through veiling and secluded existence within the *andarunn* (inner-courtyard), to taking militant part in revolution, from being forced to unveil and then reveil themselves, sent into an exploitative market place and later back to the confines of domestic life in the interest of the state, the dichotomy of the armed angel emerged.' It is important to be clear that when Mandana refers to women's secluded existence through veiling and to their existence within the *andarunn*, she refers to the condition of a minority of women in nineteenth-century Iran. As she says, during the 1850s, over 80 per cent of the population lived in the countryside and obviously had a different life from the urban 20 per cent. There is no evidence of women's seclusion in the countryside, not because they were emancipated, but because of extreme poverty and their high degree of economic activity within agricultural industries.

Another statement, which describes women's conditions in the twentieth century, reads as if the emergent dichotomy of the 'armed angel' is a description of the conditions of Iranian women within capitalism. Women, whether in developed industrial capitalist societies or in less developed ones, have always been used as instruments of state policies, despite the fact that their oppression may take different forms in relation to specific, social conditions. Women have always been encouraged to be caring angels, and, if necessary, public participants in social affairs. In Iran the instrumental position took a radical form because extreme conditions necessitated extreme measures.

The idea of the armed-angel-as-revolutionary simply explains women's condition within radical Islam and not in Iran. As Shariati advocates, and Mandana refers to: 'The comparison was made with the two Moslem heroines of the past – the armed ones and the angel Zeinub and Fatima – by Ali-Shariati who transformed these symbols of suffering and helplessness in the hostile world into active revolutionaries who fought for social justice.' It is within radical Islam that women are encouraged to be devoted wives and selfless mothers, while at the same time expected to take up arms and get directly involved in political life. Therefore, the name of Mandana's booklet is not appropriate as a description of the condition of Iranian women in general.

Finally, Mandana looks at the dual responsibilities of Iranian women which are guaranteed by the principle of *Velazat-e-Fagih*. She discusses the role played by women during the Gulf War where they have been used to serve the war industries in paid and unpaid labour, and have been instruments of propaganda for the regime, portrayed as symbols of devotion and sacrifice. This, in fact, has been used to challenge those critical of the Islamic regime.

Women's condition within the

family is also discussed as a means of controlling their social and sexual behaviour. Mandana argues that the implication of *Muta* (temporary marriage) and the function of *Bonzade-e-Ezdevag* (foundation of marriage) are critically important in understanding the forms of sexuality imposed on women. She explores the implications of all forms of law as part of the government's systematic attack on women's rights.

She concludes by arguing that despite the absolute deterioration of their legal and social rights, women are seen and recognized as too important socially and economically to be ignored; yet the burden of being the domestic worker, selfless worker and devoted wife is the reality of women's life in Iran today. She believes that: 'unless women reject the enforced ideology of armed angel and take full control over their lives, they will never be fully emancipated'.

I would like to add that the precondition for women's emancipation is not only the rejection of the ideology of armed angel, but also the demand for a new division of labour and the responsibilities of childcare, the disappearance of all forms of actual and assumed dependence on the male wage, and the transformation of the ideology of gender and sexuality.

Armed Angels is full of substantial and stimulating material. It covers the most dynamic period of Iranian history. I finished it feeling that such an informative piece of work has been long overdue. I recommend the work to anyone interested in knowing about the past and present conditions of Iranian women.

Elham

Note

Armed Angels is available from CHANGE, P.O. Box 824, London SE24 9JS. Telephone: 071 277 6187

Seductions: Studies in Reading and Culture
Jane Miller
Virago: London, 1990 ISBN 0 86068 943 3, £14.99 Pbk

Kate Millett's broadside against Normal Mailer, Henry Miller, and other gurus of twentieth-century sexual and political radicalism and flagrant traducers of women gave us, in *Sexual Politics*, one of the founding texts of feminism's 'second wave'. Subsequent Anglo-American literary criticism preferred to recover and study women's writing. Jane Miller's *Seductions* returns the spotlight on to another kind of male-authored text: works of theory in which women are not so much traduced as ignored: four key writers whose work has profoundly affected the development of twentieth-century cultural studies: Antonio Gramsci, Raymond Williams, Edward Said and Mikhail Bakhtin.

We might, of course, return the compliment and ignore what radical feminism has termed 'malestream theory'; but not without loss. Miller's strategy is rather to engage with these writers, countering them not, or not only, in their own terms but by drawing on less abstract forms of writing which have sometimes been claimed for women and feminism: fiction, biography, personal writing.

Seductions, as befits its title, is engaging, subtle, charming, disarming – a good read. It progresses not in a straight line dictated by an argument, but laterally, with loups and detours. We are treated, for example, within the confines of a chapter whose main theme is the significance of Gramsci's concept of hegemony, to a comparison between two eighteenth-century literary seducers: Richardson's Lovelace and

Jane Austen's Willoughby. We are given snippets of autobiography as Jane Miller reflects on her own experience as a student at Cambridge, a young mother, a niece. And at the centre of her book we have the figure of her great-aunt Clara Collet, who was not the prototype for Gissings formidable 'new woman' Rhoda Nunn, but was certainly her equal and her likeness. She was a civil servant in the late nineteenth and early twentieth centuries, living like a man in chambers, and, like her literary counterpart, with more than a hint of austere masculinity about her.

The features of the terrain explored by the book are made visible through the guiding metaphor of seduction. Seduction rather than hegemony is chosen to characterize women's relationship to cultures that both include and simultaneously exclude us. Miller's argument is that we are seduced into ambivalent assent to our own domination through myriad temptations. Any one of them may be resisted; but ultimately we merely choose between them.

Women in patriarchal capitalism are, in Gramsci's term, subaltern: inferior: of subordinate rank; but also, in the context of logical categories, *particular* rather than general or universal. But abstract theorizing refuses particularity in a 'lofty . . . tradition of philosopher kings . . . for whom the sexlessness of important ideas and of thought itself is axiomatic, and whose style expresses only genial disapproval of an attention to differences between women and men.' (4) Subaltern woman cannot escape her sex, her particularity; hegemonic man is unable or unwilling to see himself and his theory as gendered.

So, Miller proceeds by teasing out gender-absences (and equally telling presences) as metaphor. Thus on Said: 'Within these anti-imperialist discourses it is women's vulnerabilities and the injuries they attract to themselves which become metaphors for the injuries suffered by whole societies and for the consequent humiliations of their men' (120), in the work of these theorists. But she counterposes them not with critique, modification, reworking: the work of feminist theorizing; but with women's words in other, more particularizing forms of writing: Gramsci's hegemony is set alongside narratives of seduction and betrayal; Williams's working-class male romance with Carolyn Steedman's biographical and autobiographical landscape; Said's metaphor of colonial feminization with Toni Morrison's *Beloved*; Bakhtin's Rabelasian carnival with Margaret Atwood's *Cat's Eye*, and the hesitations of a young black A-level student in the face of the demands of a syllabus and a way of reading which excludes her experience; and at the centre, with a woman's life.

Miller makes the metaphor go a long way, and she uses it to make some telling points. Yet like all metaphors it may be pushed too far. Used to stand for the form of women's incorporation into the gendered mainstream of social life it is not quite right. For this is a stepping *into* femininity, into all-too licit heterosexual marriage. But she who allows herself to be seduced steps outside the bounds of propriety, to partake of illicit pleasures – to yield, deliciously, recklessly, to temptation.

Seduction bespeaks transgression, and Miller's main use of the term is to characterize feminists' relationship to transgressive theories aimed at laying bare modes of cultural domination. Miller writes of such theorizing as 'perhaps one of the deadliest and least resistable of seductions for feminists' (8).

These are strong words. Yet there is something not quite right here either. To be seduced is to succumb to overwhelming temptation against one's better judgement. It implies an active if duplicitous wooing. Yet our plaint was of neglect. It is feminism, therefore, that must take the active part in forging any relationships with these theories, determining the terms on which they are entered. Feminists who have drawn on them may rightly want to object to a metaphor which suggests an unprincipled, total, and passive mental yielding. If we have been seduced, then this must be shown through analysis of the uses made of those theories by feminists.

Terry Lovell

Heroes of Their Own Lives: The Politics and History of Family Violence
Linda Gordon
Virago: London, 1989
ISBN 1 85381 039 8, £11.99 Pbk

As a survivor of family violence I was attracted to Linda Gordon's book from the start. Here, I hoped, would be a coherent study that would put the issues into a clear historical and political context. I have always held Gordon's work in high regard and was pleased that it was she who should tackle this minefield of theoretical and methodological problems. In many ways I have not been disappointed: it is a very good study. In another way, however, I have serious reservations.

The research is based on case records from three social-welfare agencies in Boston between 1870 and 1980. Using case records in this way is an innovative approach. They are analyzed lucidly with extracts from written and photographic records. Major stages of the growth and professionalization of welfare agencies are charted, and there is a particularly good chapter on the contradictions and 'double binds' which plagued single mothers. Throughout, Gordon pays careful attention to gender issues, both with reference to the social-work agencies and to their clients.

Gordon's central thesis is that family violence, and definitions of family violence, have been historically and politically constructed.

This is an important riposte to sociobiological and psychological theories which dominated the field for some time. She illustrates, for example, how the initial definition of 'child cruelty' became redefined as 'child neglect', as a result of which blame shifted from fathers to mothers. 'Moral panics' such as we have witnessed at Cleveland are, she argues, seldom about any actual numerical increase in abuse, but rather about wider political crises.

The title betrays the other central aim of the book: to obviate simple social-control theories about welfare policies and to highlight and applaud women's *agency*: 'one of the most striking findings of this study is how often the objects of social control themselves asked for intervention from child-protection agencies' (6). She argues that family members negotiate power among themselves and turn to agencies to help in their problems. This is why she rejects the use of patriarchy as a concept, except in its limited meaning of traditional father-headed households.

What troubled me most, however, was the way in which Gordon draws general conclusions from a limited and quite narrow data source. The case records are all based on social workers' representations of the poor and destitute. That in itself is a problem which Joan Scott takes up elsewhere (*Signs* Vol. 15, No. 4, Summer 1990). Gordon generalizes about family violence *overall* as if poverty and family violence were, and are, inextricably connected. While not wishing to contest that much family violence does correlate with poverty, I do want to make clear that not all family violence, by any means, does, and that, of course, not all the poor have violent families.

To digress to my own childhood: I grew up in the USA in the 1950s. My parents were middle-class WASPs. Poverty was never an issue for us, yet there was a great deal of family violence – primarily incest, inflicted by my father. Rape and abuse, however, were not named as such, but were hidden in secrecy. The experiences were repressed, buried deep in the unconscious. We were never seen as, or defined as, an abusive or even a problem family: no discourses existed for middle-class families such as ours at that time. Because there was no language, direct resistance was impossible. Certainly, heroism was out of the question. My resistance took the path of school phobia and epilepsy. The problem became medicalized and psychiatrized. I became the problem.

In other words, some family violence had, and has, nothing to do with poverty. I think, in my case, it had *something* to do with psychology. I think it had even more to do with a number of discourses which were current at that time: while my mother was reading D. H. Lawrence and *Fear of Freedom*, my father was reading *Lolita* and *The Bad Seed*. Songs like 'My Heart Belongs to Daddy' were popular. Freud, of course, had provided the perfect cover for male violence. My father gave my sister a book about the Oedipus complex for her thirteenth birthday. Regardless of my own past, there is now a great deal of evidence that incest is not a class-specific phenomenon.

Of course, there is very little historical data about family violence and using case records is an interesting way to explore some of the issues. But to generalize from these is to misrepresent both the poor and family violence. It bolsters a recurring tendency to locate family violence, but especially incest, 'out there'. Professionals acknowledged its existence for a long time, but as something that existed elsewhere: among the poor, or immigrants, or in rural backwaters, never in one's own backyard. Largely as a result of second-wave feminism and important revisions of psychoanalytical theory, these assumptions have now been well and truly challenged. Gordon, I am sure unwittingly, brings us dangerously close to them again by correlating family violence with poverty in this way.

But if social class cannot explain family violence, could patriarchy? Most family violence is male violence, and this is disguised by the term '"family" violence'. Although mothers do abuse children, as Gordon shows, it is significantly less and is rarely sexualized. If patriarchy is defined as both an age and a gender relationship it might be more useful. Although admittedly universalistic and transhistorical, at least it does convey a sense of the way in which family violence is strongly gendered. Patriarchy, rightly politicizes it.

Poststructuralist theory is another way into the problem. Social-welfare discourse on families and violence was only one among several – although certainly the most relevant to the poor. In the case of incest, psychiatric discourse labelled it as fantasy. Books like *Lolita* extolled and eroticized sexual abuse of girls; books like *The Bad Seed* helped lay the blame firmly on to girls themselves. Representations of women in films, TV and advertising made them 'kittenish', babylike and further confused and conflated boundaries between women and children by both sexualizing girls and 'enchilding' women.

The problem with poststructuralist theory, however, is that it doesn't leave adequate conceptual space for power and power relations. All discourses are equal but some are more equal than others. They explain a lot, but not, for instance, why my mother spent twenty years in a mental hospital, where she died, while my father, who became a professor of science, lives a life of luxury retirement in Florida. Discourse doesn't tell us enough about men's privileged positions, it doesn't explain why and how certain discourses carry more weight, more cogency than others.

It seems to me that no one theory has yet adequately accounted for family violence. It needs to be broken down into smaller conceptual categories. Ironically, Gordon *does* do just this, and does it well, but then lumps them all together under the rubric of 'family violence'. Yet incest and wife-beating, child neglect and child-battering cannot necessarily be explained in similar ways. What is clear is that they need much more research and thought before any one theoretical paradigm can be used to explain them all. I suggest that what may be needed is a new paradigm altogether. Linda Gordon's book has made an excellent and pioneering start to this project.

Diana Gittins

Unruly Practices: Power, Discourse and Gender in Contemporary Social Theory
Nancy Fraser

Polity Press in association with Basil Blackwell: Oxford, 1989
ISBN 0 7456 0391 2, £8.95 Pbk;
ISBN 0 7456 0390 4 £27.50 Hbk

In her introduction to *Unruly Practices*, Nancy Fraser, the American philosopher and critical theorist, locates her work in relation to the state of American academia: 'It is fashionable nowadays to decry efforts to combine activism and academia. Neoconservatives tell us that to practice critique while employed by an education institution is a betrayal of professional standards. Conversely, some independent left-wing intellectuals insist that to join the professoriat is to betray the imperative of critique. Finally, many activists outside the academy doubt the commitment and reliability of academics who claim to be their allies and comrades in struggle' (1). These are issues also familiar to feminists outside America which often crystallize into questions of the accountability of feminist academics to the broader women's movement. Fraser's aim is to be a politically critical academic who recognizes that radicals in universities do 'find themselves subject to competing pressures and counter pressures . . . do internalise several distinct and mutually incompatible sets of expectations'. A reading of *Unruly Practices* from outside the American academic context left me wondering about the possibilities and limits of politicized critical practice in the United States. Is it possible to cross the boundaries between academic criticism and activism outside higher education? How important are questions of style, accessibility and audience? Is it enough for a socialist feminist to write in ways that assume considerable prior knowledge on the part of readers and are taxing even for other academics? Certainly there must be a space for such work but what, ultimately, are its politics?

The essays collected in *Unruly Practices* were first published in various American journals between 1981 and 1988. Divided into three sections, the essays undertake a critical engagement with various aspects of contemporary social theory. Part one deals with crucial aspects of Foucault's work: his concept of power, the question of his 'conservatism' and his 'body language'. Readers who are already familiar with Foucault's texts will find these essays interesting,

cogently argued and a useful contribution to the current debate on the
critical and political potential of Foucauldian theory. Of particular interest is Fraser's consideration of Foucault's relationship to liberal norms
of what is good and desirable and the
question of how one distinguishes
between acceptable and unacceptable forms of power. These issues are
taken up in all three essays which
also look at the status of modernity
in Foucault's work and his 'rejection'
of humanism.

Part two comprises two essays.
They examine the relation between
politics and deconstruction in the
work of the French Derrideans and
Richard Rorty's position in relation
to romanticism and technocracy.
Like the previous essays, these, too,
assume a fair degree of prior knowledge. They are specialized, yet
interesting. It is in Part Three that
Fraser moves on to consider more
directly aspects of gender in social
theory. She analyzes the gender
blindness of Habermas's 'social-
theoretical categorical framework'
and looks at the gendered nature of
definitions of need and social welfare
provisions in the United States.

It will come as little surprise to
those familiar with social theory and
feminist critiques of the welfare
state, whether in Britain or America,
to learn that different sectors of the
welfare state are gendered and that
they position women and men differently. Fraser looks at the position of
women both as recipients of welfare
programmes and as paid and unpaid
social-service workers. She highlights the counterfactual nature of
the assumptions on which welfare
provisions are based, pointing, for

example, to how 'fewer than 15 per
cent of US families conform to the
normative ideal of domicile shared
by a husband who is sole breadwin-
ner, a wife who is full-time homemaker, and their offspring' (149).
She argues that social insurance
schemes which provide unemploy-
ment benefit position recipients as
'rights-bearers' – purchasing consumers who are receiving something
for which they have paid. Other
forms of welfare provision, which are
directed primarily at women – relief
programmes, food stamps, Medicaid
and public-housing assistance – define their recipients as '"benefici-
aries of government largess" or
"clients of public charity"' and reinforce patriarchal structures (152).
Following on from this, Fraser
shows, in her final chapter, how
definitions of needs are an important
political issue for feminists.

Unruly Practices is a useful book
for students of social theory. It will
appeal to those interested in and
familiar with the work of Foucault,
Rorty and Habermas as well as readers concerned with the implications
of social theory in public policy. The
loosely connected series of essays are
clearly written, dense and demanding. The final chapters on the politics
of need-interpretation, which attempt to put theoretical insights into
practice, are perhaps the most ac-
cessible. They clearly demonstrate
that social theories do inform welfare practice and that critiques of
gendering in social theory can throw
light on how contemporary welfare
practice might be challenged.

Chris Weedon

Sexual Difference: A Theory of Social-Symbolic Practice
Milan Women's Bookstore Collective

(Translated by Patricia Cicogna and Teresa de Lauretis) *Indiana University Press: Bloomington and Indianapolis, 1990 ISBN 0 253 20605 7, £9.95 Pbk*

The major stumbling block in comprehension for a British or American feminist reading *Sexual Difference* is being confronted with familiar ideas and experiences that are combined in the most unfamiliar way. The book strongly argues for a radical separatism, based on an assumed absolute dualism between men and women ('Sexual difference is an originary human difference', p. 125). At the same time, it uses postmodernist theory in emphasizing the importance of desire, power and difference in relations between women ('The egalitarianism of our [earlier] political groups precluded the symbolic power of our differences', p. 112). It further brings feminist psychoanalysis into the argument by speaking of symbolic origins of women being based on the figure of the mother ('It was a short step . . . from accepting the fact of inequality [between women] to thinking that we get value from a female source, the mother, in a symbolic sense', p. 111).

The Milan Women's Bookstore Collective have evidently not paid much heed to the divisions between libertarians, revolutionary feminists, radical feminists and psychoanalytic feminists in this country, and socialist feminism really does not enter into the debate at all. Nor, for that matter, do they pay any attention to the splits between lesbian feminists and heterosexual feminists, and nor do they attend to race, class or disability in their treatment of difference. Despite that, the book is useful, as it unsettles any pre-set notions that there are basic underlying contradictions between these different strands of feminist thought, or that there is a pre-ordained pattern for the development of feminist debates. It highlights the fact, if this needed any further highlighting, that cultural contexts matter a great deal. The book was originally written in Italian, for Italian feminists. It therefore did not need to explain its own context, leaving the English-speaking reader with the uneasy sense that the ideas are at once both familiar and unfamiliar. That does not make it easy reading, and leads one to ponder whether British and American texts are equally mystifying to the Italians.

The difficulties are compounded by frequent references to what appears to be a large portion of the contents of the Milan Women's Bookstore. To those unfamiliar with much classical women's literature, developments in postmodernist thought, as well as Western philosophy, the book will be hard going. Notions of the social contract, concepts of justice, freedom and equality are dealt with in a manner which assumes the reader is already familiar with the debates surrounding them.

In its stated intention, *Sexual Difference* sets out to chart the development of this brand of feminist theory from the practice and experience of a particular group of women. It is grounded, therefore, on outlining the links between theory and practice and reconstructing how the ideas set forth in the book came to be formulated. As such, much of the book is devoted to summarizing the contents of various feminist newsletters and conferences, pointing to moments at which changes in understanding occurred. Here one is often on familiar ground, where discussions of the experience of consciousness-raising groups, abortion and antirape campaigns, the running of women-only spaces and the pain of disputes arising in feminist conferences sound all too familiar. But rarely do actual women appear in these accounts except as authors or as examples of a woman's experience. Certainly, the authors of *Sexual Difference* themselves do not appear. Thus, despite being based on practice, the book still relies heavily on theory and texts, concentrating more on the abstract ideas which were the outcome of moments of practice than on describing the actual activities themselves.

Sexual Difference bases its underlying analysis on looking at the relations between women, not on the relations between men and women. It argues that there is no point in looking at the relations between men and women, because women had no hand in defining them, and women will not find their own freedom there: 'Women do not owe anything to men . . . [a woman] owes, instead, to other women – to the one who brought her into the world, to those who have loved her, those who have taught her something, those who have spent their energies to make the world more comfortable for her. . . . The female price for freedom is the payment of this symbolic debt.' (129)

The most startling aspect of the book, and its major argument, is its complete rejection of the idea that all women should, in an ideal world, be equal. The authors insist that the desire for equality is based on a misplaced understanding of women's oppression within a male-defined sociality. In fighting for women's rights, feminists in the past insisted on the equally oppressed nature of all women, and thus their 'equality' was based on women being victims. In other words, the book argues that the notion of 'equality' was founded upon what men said women were; this notion of equality was still based on accepting the ideas of a society which had been defined and constructed without women in mind. Therefore, women will never achieve freedom while trying to achieve this kind of 'equality'. The

book argues that, as the authors discovered in women's collectives, women are demonstrably not equal. Rather than try and deny this inequality, it should be used to build women's own freedom. The insistence on equality, they say, prevented women from recognizing the true source of their freedom: other women, from whom one can learn what only women can teach.

This is where the notion of the 'mother' and 'entrustment' arises. Women have to give other women the authority, they argue, to teach them. The obvious symbolic metaphor for this relationship of 'entrustment' for the authors is the mother–daughter relationship. Through accepting this authority from another woman one can achieve, it seems, freedom.

The book comes up against conceptual snares which have been experienced elsewhere. Its biggest difficulty is attempting to assert women's 'originary' difference from men, without ever saying exactly what this difference is, while at the same time asserting absolute difference *between* women. If women are all different, then what is it that makes them the 'same'? In what sense is their gender 'originary'? We are told that a woman's experience, 'has intrinsic authenticity. That authenticity is . . . absolute, in the sense that there is no possible authenticity for women except in what they experience themselves' (42). This cannot be questioned. It must be accepted. But if the authors accept the socially constructed nature of a man's world, and agree that women must socially construct their own world, amongst women themselves, then whence the 'originary' difference? It has to be asserted for, otherwise, if the only reality is a constructed reality, the new women's world can only be based on what women already know about sociality. And, as the authors say, the sociality they have experienced is a masculine one. This is the fundamental difficulty in all feminist theories which argue that women constitute a 'muted group',[1] a group with no language of its own and no society of its own. Despite the useful sideways glances given to the notions of difference and inequality between women provided for an English-speaking reader, this fundamental conundrum was not, in the end, surmounted.

Sarah Green

Note

1 The phrase was first coined by Edwin Ardener, 'The problem revisited', in S. Ardener (ed.), *Perceiving Women*, London: Dent, 1975, pp. 19–27.

The Condition of Women in France: 1945 to the Present. A Documentary Anthology
Edited by Claire Laubier
Routledge: London, 1990
ISBN 0 415 03091 9, £7.99 Pbk

Claire Laubier's anthology, aimed at the A-level or undergraduate student of French as well as the general reader, is structured both chronologically and thematically, and each chapter contains an introduction in English to the French texts. With the exception of the chapter devoted to de Beauvoir's *The Second Sex*, the first five chapters take us through the decades from 1945 to 1980, while the final four chapters are devoted to thematic areas: language; work, politics and power; home life; and contemporary women's writing. This structure makes it very easy to use the book selectively as a source of material as well as in its entirety, and it would be particularly convenient to direct students to particular chapters or texts relevant to their own interests or the course they are following.

The introductions to each chapter provide a clear and concise overview, and the chapters devoted to particular decades manage to convey something of the cultural climate of the period as well as information; this is particularly true for the 1950s, where the inclusion of examples of the iconography of the period in the form of advertisements and film stills lends a further dimension to the texts and opens up interesting possibilities for classroom exploitation. The other chapters are perhaps slightly lacking in visual material, and it is a pity that at least some of the texts have not been reproduced in their original format, given the current emphasis on authenticity in language teaching, and the useful clues to comprehension which textual layout can provide.

It seems highly appropriate that a whole chapter is devoted to what is arguably one of the most important and influential feminist works to be published since the war – de Beauvoir's *The Second Sex* – and the inclusion of reviews of the book from the period is invaluable as a means of contextualizing the work, and of enabling students in the 1990s to realize just how revolutionary it was at the time of publication. The chapter on the women's movement from 1968–80 does not develop the analysis of de Beauvoir's influence, but it does provide a clear and very useful summary of the main tendencies and of issues addressed by French feminists in the 1970s.

It is also appropriate that a whole chapter is devoted to language, given the particular problems posed for feminist writers by a language whose grammatical structure reinforces gender inequality more obviously than that of a less inflected language such as English, and the considerable importance which as a result has been attached to issues of language by feminists in France; in this chapter the focus is mainly on the work of sociolinguists such as

Marina Yaguello and of socialist reformers such as Yvette Roudy, and we must turn to the chapter on women's writing for a discussion of the ways in which writers of contemporary fiction are preoccupied with the language question. This introduction to contemporary women's writing is refreshing in that, although it raises the issue of 'feminine writing', it introduces writers who with the possible exception of Duras and Sarraute are less well known outside France than theorists and exponents of the 'feminine' text such as Irigaray and Cixous. Although Laubier's choice of texts does not stray far outside the literary canon, the textual extracts do give some indication of the wealth of women's writing in France which does not conform to the avant-garde, highly theoretical image of French feminism frequently predominant in anglophone contexts.

The chapter on 'home life' is, as its title might suggest, the most problematic, since neither the introduction or textual extracts make any reference to lesbians in France, and even single women are only mentioned in passing. The extracts chosen are all interviews with married or widowed women, who express conventional liberal views of the role of women within marriage and the family. This may be indicative of a greater ideological dominance of the ideologies of romantic love and of the family in French culture, but the extracts are unfortunately not framed by a contexualizing discussion of this issue. Some investigation of the lives of single women in France, building on Evelyne Le Garrec's fascinating compilation of interviews, *Un lit à soi* (A Bed of One's Own[1]) (1979) is long overdue and, while this is clearly beyond the scope of Claire Laubier's book, some discussion of employment and housing issues for single women, as well as acknowledgement that single women have home lives too, would

have helped to counterbalance the French cultural ethos referred to above.

The complete exclusion of lesbians from this chapter, and indeed from the whole anthology is, to say the least, controversial in a work which is claiming historical veracity, and the ideological implications are depressingly clear. This is evidently a serious problem from the pedagogic point of view, and most feminist teachers would as a result find this material, however useful, incomplete; in recent classes on the private sphere in France, for instance, I did find some of the statistics in the 'home life' chapter useful, but only alongside information on lesbian and gay relationships from *Rapport gai: enquête sur les modes de vie homosexuels*, an interesting survey published by les Editions Persona (1984).

A further problematic absence is the situation of ethnic groups in France. Although the impact of the Algerian war on French political life is discussed, the lives of the large numbers of North African women who are first- and second-generation immigrants in France remain undocumented in this anthology, and the chapter on the women's movement, perhaps because it in fact stops in 1980 and not the present day, does not mention organizations such as 'Les Nanas Beurs' formed by second-generation North African immigrants or 'MODEFEN' (Movement for the Defence of Black Women's Rights).

With these exclusions and the resulting need to supplement the material in mind, there is no doubt that Claire Laubier has produced an interesting and useful anthology, which feminist teachers of French will welcome as a refreshing change from the usual 'one chapter on women' format so typical of the French language textbook.

Lyn Thomas

Note

1 This is my own translation of the title –
the book has not been translated into
English.

References

CAVAILHES, Jean, DUTEY, Pierre and BACH-

IGNASSE, Gerard (1984) *Rapport gai:
enquête sur les modes de vie homosexuels* Paris: Editions Persona.
LE GARREC, Evelyne (1979) *Un lit à soi*
Paris: Editions du Seuil.

The World is Ill Divided: Women's Work in Scotland in the Nineteenth and Early Twentieth Centuries

Eleanor Gordon and Esther
Breitenbach

Edinburgh University Press: 1990
ISBN 0 7486 0116 3, £25.00 Hbk.
ISBN 0 7486 0212 7 £11.95 Pbk.

This volume of essays forms part of
an Edinburgh Education and Society
Series. It represents a welcome addition to our understanding of the
history of British women's waged
work and a challenge to its frequent
anglocentrism, constituting an important step in the belated yet now
burgeoning fields of Scottish, Welsh
and Irish women's history. Three
recent books on Scotland are by
women involved in this volume (Eleanor Gordon, 1991; Linda Mahood,
1990; Siân Reynolds, 1989).

The eight essays are consistently concise and clearly organized
with brief bibliographies, making
them especially appealing for students although they are a bit uneven
– a few become rather immersed in
detail. A useful Introduction pulls
together the main themes, drawing
attention to the persistence of gender divisions in employment and
limited choices for women, but resisting simplistic ideas of women as
mere victims of circumstance. Oral
history helps challenge many received notions. The concentration on
the twentieth century does however
slightly belie the book's subtitle with

only two essays centrally addressing
the bulk of the nineteenth century.
Possibly because of this imbalance,
the book does not follow a broadly
chronological pattern. This is
slightly confusing since, for example,
the reader shifts from 1910 to 1950
in the opening essay, back to the
nineteenth century then forward
again to Edwardian Scotland by the
third essay. Uniting them, however,
is a concern with a gendered division
of labour and how this shaped
women's lives and prospects at different times and in varying places
and occupations.

Linda Mahood's exploration of
Victorian Magdalen homes in Glasgow and Edinburgh raises important
questions about moral regulation,
the definition and control of sexu-
alities and the shaping of ideas about
working-class respectability. The di-
rectors reconciled their worries
about women's employment with the
need for these 'unfortunates' to work
for the homes and provided not only
'women fit for work, but work fit for
women'. The other essay on Victorian Scotland examines the women
out-workers or bondagers in the
south-east, tracing the decline of the
system and the particular vulner-
ability and powerlessness of those
working for their families. Not surprisingly, given the paucity of evidence from the women themselves,
much of our knowledge of the system
is refracted through the perceptions
of the male farmworkers/relatives,
the ploughman or hind.

In contrast, the essay on
women's memories of work in Stirling in the first half of this century

draws on eighty women's memories in the Stirling Women's Oral History Archive. It challenges the notion that working-class women defined themselves essentially through their domestic life, arguing that most of these women enjoyed their working lives. Yet enjoyment need not connote freedom from exploitation. Moreover, the authors do not question how far the quality of life (or, rather, lack of it) in the present might help determine the way the women remember the past. Lynn Jamieson's piece on rural and urban women in domestic service earlier this century examines this wide-ranging job from both employees' and employers' memories, warning against an image of total gloom and doom. Even some urban women seem to have viewed some of their experiences in a positive light and sometimes opted for service in preference to other limited openings. Oral history has also been used in the essay on Prinlaws, a Fifeshire textile village, concentrating on young women's employment between the wars and questioning their independence, showing how they remained very much under parental control. Some discussion of whether the group interviews might have prompted particular collective responses could have been illuminating.

Alice J. Albert's essay focuses on home-workers who tended to be married women. Her work on Glasgow sweated home-workers between 1875 and 1914 traces the deterioration of their prospects, showing them struggling for work in a diminishing market. Another essay on Glasgow addresses a much more privileged group, 62 early women medical graduates. Wendy Alexander shatters several preconceptions, revealing a wider social background than comfortable middle class and showing that despite gender-based obstacles in appointments and promotion, over 88 per cent practised after graduation for

either a considerable period or a lifetime, with many marrying and continuing their work. Skilled workers were also the subject of Siân Reynold's essay which examines the fluctuations in women's fortunes as compositors and bookbinders as part of her study of Edwardian employment in the printing and paper trades. Her account of disputes within the trades shows not only how women's work was delimited but also sensitivity towards exploring some of the perceptions men and women had of each other as workers and hence their misgivings.

The editors acknowledge class and regional diversity *within* Scotland. They also make a disclaimer, stating that the essays do not attempt 'to elucidate or define the distinctiveness of Scottish women's experience'. This is understandable since it would have involved engagement in a complex debate not entirely central to the book's aims. Yet it seems a pity that it was not tackled at all. For example, the essay on home-workers stresses that in Scotland (and especially in Glasgow) the conjugal family cannot be seen as the focus for domestic production. Unlike in England, women tended to work alone or in small groups. What factors might have contributed to this? Some brief introductory discussion of the possible impact of indigenous economic and cultural factors and, in particular, the part played by Scottish legal and educational developments in helping shape the attitudes and experiences of women workers in Scotland could have been instructive for readers. Nevertheless, this is a stimulating book with a wealth of fascinating material.

Angela V. John

References

GORDON, Eleanor (1991) *Women and the Labour Movement in Scotland 1850–1914* Oxford: Oxford University Press.

MAHOOD, Linda (1990) *The Magdalens: Prostitution in Scotland*, London: Routledge & Kegan Paul.

REYNOLDS, Siân (1989) *Britannica's Type-setters. Women Compositors in Edwardian Edinburgh* Edinburgh: Edinburgh University Press.

Correct Distance
Mitra Tabrizian
Cornerhouse Publications: Manchester, 1990
ISBN 0 948797 16 9, £12.95 Hbk

Correct Distance is a book *of* photographs, but it is also a book *about* photographs; about the politics of representation. Its contribution to debates within culture and representation can be traced to an earlier moment at the beginning of the eighties.

Towards the end of his introduction to *Thinking Photography* Victor Burgin stated: 'It remains for me to explain an absence. There are no essays by women in this anthology. This is a matter neither of oversight nor prejudice. It is the contingent effect of a conjuncture' (1982: 14). Burgin explained that work such as Laura Mulvey's on film, or Griselda Pollock's on painting, was not specifically photographic and Jo Spence's photographic work belonged to a different cultural–political project. None the less, he acknowledged the importance of the women's movement's insistence on the politics of representation.

The particular historical conjuncture which marked the publication of *Thinking Photography* was the post-68 emergence of a critical photographic practice and criticism which was theoretically informed by Marxism, structuralism and psychoanalysis. *Thinking Photography* made available to photographers and cultural historians new perspectives which radically challenged traditional understandings of the medium.

Correct Distance by Mitra Tabrizian represents a significant development of these ideas from the perspective of sexual and cultural difference. (Mitra Tabrizian is an Iranian woman living in London). While *Thinking Photography* brought together essays published between 1970 and 1980, *Correct Distance* presents photographic work and articles about representation made during the following decade.

In her introduction to *Correct Distance*, Griselda Pollock traces the shift within feminist interventions in visual culture which took place in the intervening years. Increasingly, questions of pleasure, desire and identity became important. 'Radical cultural practice of the seventies seemed to experience the weight of regulative ideological power in culture and hence felt the need to practice a negative deconstructive aesthetic as a strategy of resistance.' (Pollock in Tabrizian, 1990) But by the eighties what had emerged was something 'less disciplined by a practice of disidentification and negation and more willing to address the power of fantasy and the destabilising force of pleasure.' (Pollock in Tabrizian, 1991)

Correct Distance offers a map of the ways in which the debate on sexual difference and photographic practice developed during the eighties. It is through this broader feminist project, with its emphasis on the *sexual* politics of representation and the questions of desire and pleasure, that the work should be read. The eighties saw an explosion of feminist cultural publishing which has made work more widely available. One of the most significant contributions of feminism has been the refusal to accept traditional disciplinary boundaries. Its task, rather, has been to trace the discourses of femininity as a means of understanding how 'woman' is not only socially and culturally but also psychically produced (and only has meaning in re-lation to the term 'man'). Thus Mitra Tabrizian's work draws upon the conventions of photography and film, on popular and mass culture, on semiological, structuralist, psycho-analytic as well as feminist theories.

If, since the 1980s, psychoanaly-sis has had particular importance for feminism, then it is firstly because of the realization that the view of femi-ninity as either biologically deter-mined or simply socially constructed was inadequate. The unconscious, like the term 'difference', represents a space *between* the biological and the social which is not reducible to either. Secondly, as Victor Burgin has said elsewhere, the whole point about ideology is that it is not a matter of false consciousness, nor even a matter of consciousness. Ideology is profoundly unconscious. In this volume, five pieces of work are reproduced which trace these debates. The first two, 'College of Fashion' (1980–1) and 'Governmen-tality' (1981–2), represent an in-vestigation into fashion and adver-tising as two of the primary sites for the construction of gender and sub-jectivity. Both use black-and-white documentary photography but the images are accompanied by text drawn from different discourses. It is between these two symbolic systems in the space between image and text that meaning is produced: 'represen-tations are neither reducible to a referent outside . . . nor to an origin in a subject.' (Tabrizian, 'Govern-mentality', 1982)

The last two works, 'The Blues' (1986–7), on the complexities of race, gender and class and 'Surveillance' (1988–9), a recent history of Tab-rizian's native Iran, both raise other questions and present perspectives which challenge the dominance of the West. In one image from 'The Blues' entitled 'Double Edge' two men (one black, one white) stand on either side of a door. The black man holds a piece of paper on which is written: 'Your problem is you want to be in two places at once. You want everything the whites have got. And you want to destroy everything the

From *Correct Distance* by Mitra Tabrizian

whites have got. My problem is that I'm the woman of no colour. Does that make us different or the same?' (Tabrizian, 'The Blues', 1987)

The questions of race and history and their complex relation to gender have become increasingly important. The final work, 'Surveillance', takes the form of a panorama and, unlike the earlier work which examines a synchronic layering of femininity, it is diachronic in structure.

Pivotal to these arguments, placed between the two sets of earlier and later work and providing the book's title, is the centrepiece of the book: 'Correct Distance'.

In 'Correct Distance' (1984–5) the style of *film noir* with its *femme fatale* comes to represent an underworld, a dark place, a dark continent: the place of the unconscious and woman. It is also the place where the rigid binary oppositions of male and female have not yet formed. In the fictive space of the cinema, or within the photograph's frame, the spectator like the infant can move between active and passive identification. The *femme fatale* represents a powerful figure both desired and feared. Within the narrative, the price she must pay for both appropriating masculinity and reminding the male of his feminine side is that she will be punished, forced to submit to the law and returned to her place within a system of binary opposites.

The problem here is precisely one of achieving the 'correct distance': 'far enough not to awaken the man's secret and dangerous identification . . . yet close enough not to let the feminine side be forgotten' (Tabrizian, 'Correct Distance', 1985). This also takes us back to the opening page of Tabrizian's book where a quote taken from Levi-Strauss's *Structural Anthropology* appears: 'It would be better if you went upstream and built your own village, for our customs are somewhat different

from yours. Not knowing each other's ways, the young men might have differences and there would be wars. Do not go too far away, for people who live far apart are like strangers and wars break out between them. Travel north only until you cannot see the smoke from our lodges and there build your village. Then we will be close enough to be friends and not far enough away to be enemies.' (Levi-Strauss, 1972: 254–5) It is the symbolic – culture, language, representation – which places us in relation to others and which gives us a sense of place in the world and the ability to speak and be understood by others.

While in *Correct Distance* the reference is primarily to the difference between men and women, it stands as a metaphor for all difference – cultural, sexual and racial. It is a testament to the need for the other and, as the unconscious constantly reminds us, the other is not only outside, elsewhere, but within ourselves.

Within feminist practice the question of distance and closeness, the need for analytic frameworks while not rejecting 'the feminine side', remain urgent political issues. In the no man's land between the two camps, feminism has sought to challenge those binary oppositions which have constrained us within all too narrow definitions of what it means to be a woman and, more importantly, have constrained us all – men and women – within too narrow definitions of what it means to be human.

Roberta McGrath

References

BURGIN, Victor (1982) editor, *Thinking Photography* London: Macmillan.
LEVI-STRAUSS, Claude (1972) *Structural Anthropology* 2 Harmondsworth: Penguin.

Troubled Pleasures: Writing on Politics, Gender and Hedonism

Kate Soper

Verso: London, 1990
ISBN 0 86091 313 9 £32.95 Hbk;
ISBN 0 86091 536 0 £10.95 Pbk

> It was an act of stealth
> And troubled pleasure
> (Wordsworth's *Prelude*)

Pleasure is troubled. Troubled not only because many of life's pleasures involve aspects of pain and anxiety, or because the conditions within which moments of pleasure are experienced are themselves frequently fraught, but also because many of what were previously simple needs and pleasures (for food, recreation, travel) have become problematic because of the ways in which we satisfy them; ways which are ecologically damaging, morally undesirable, politically unacceptable. For modernity's definition of pleasure is itself problematic: pleasure conceived as individualistic, materialist and narcissistic. This is Soper's assertion. In making it, she is aware that she may be occupying the unpopular and unglamorous position of self-righteous puritanism. As she acknowledges: 'asking others to be troubled by their pleasures . . . is itself troubling'.

Do things not cease to be pleasurable if we must first consider whether they are compatible with the realization of full democracy, social justice and ecological responsibility? Or can we develop new forms of pleasure and sensuality which are, ultimately, less destructive and exploitative, less troubled? And can we do so without appearing to be boring old moralists? Soper wants to argue that we can, and must: and, I think, convincingly and importantly so.

For satisfaction of the pleasures of some impacts on the fulfilment of the needs of others. Discussion of the politics of needs has traditionally fallen into two distinct paradigms, the liberal and the Marxist; the former claiming that individuals must be the arbiters of their own needs; the latter claiming that the needs which people express through purchasing power are not natural, but are false needs generated by the needs of the economy. Neither of these models, claims Soper, is acceptable: for neither draws a distinction between objective and political needs; between basic human requirements (for food, health, shelter, affection) and needs not just for survival, but for human flourishing and happiness.

This becomes of political import in the recognition that we must question current satisfaction of 'first world' needs, challenge our patterns of consumption and recognize that only if we begin to enjoy ourselves rather differently can the needs of others begin to be satisfied. Furthermore, argues Soper, if we are to witness a growth in support for socialism, it will be because needs other than those for material consumption have become prominent. But is the questioning of the enjoyments of first-world affluence really about 'need' at all? Surely we are talking not of needs, but of desires?

The epistemological and methodological basis from which Soper raises these questions is the key to understanding their form and resolution. It is a thoughtful basis, delicately drawn among a morass of other, frequently more solid, positions. For Soper maintains a Marxist conviction in the need to reject the capitalist mode of production, but adopts humanist accounts of subjectivity and agency. She has sympathy with the postmodern rejection of the Enlightenment confidence in truth and progress, but draws on phenomenological and existential arguments rather than postmodernist deconstruction, for her conception of subjectivity. Thus it is that she finds more in common with de Beauvoir's perspective of 'in-difference' than with the claims of separatism, difference or hyper-individualism so dominant in recent feminist writings. In short, Soper hovers enigmatically between many of the more accepted theoretical positions of the day.

Furthermore, her theoretical stance is grounded in a commitment to philosophical realism and a rejection of those arguments which view language, art or text as constituting a primary realm of human experience. Mapping a path between determinism and radical relativism, Soper wants to adopt a dialetical perspective which perceives us to be part creators of the conditions which also to some extent create us. Hence Soper takes on board the critiques of rationality and objectivity without endorsing the triumph of irrationalism and relativism; she accepts the challenges to previously dominant analyses of power structures without falling into a position of theoretical impotence.

Postmodernist deconstruction has created an agenda in which socialism looks authoritarian in its imposition on subjects and naive in its assumption that such subjects exist. In an effort to rectify this situation, Soper hints at an alternative body of thought, situated between the affirmation of moral autonomy and the powers of historical agency; a tradition of socialist humanism. What these humanists share in common, despite their many differences, is their rejection of deterministic interpretations of historical materialism and of positivistic metaphysics and the stress placed on the active and creative component of human agency.

Soper effectively questions the validity of the Marxist rejection of 'moralism', and asserts the distinction between advocating moralism (assuming that adherence to moral values is in itself sufficient to their realization) and upholding morality. A Marxist humanist morality would involve accepting responsibility not only for how we act individually within a given system, but also for the system itself in which we participate, a 'two-tier' morality. In an age of impending nuclear catastrophe, of massive economic exploitation and ecological destruction, there is something immoral about the refusal to extend the domain of the 'moral' beyond interpersonal relations.

Soper argues for this concern with morality, not only in opposition to a Marxist rejection of moralism, but also in contradistinction to the postmodernist disinterest in ethical issues – a new variation of the long-standing equivocation around issues of morality within left-wing theory. Her claim is that Marxists and post-structuralists alike must acknowledge that their critiques of prevailing rationalities rest on an appeal to subjective freedom, a recognition that selves are not totally determined, that 'there is a self which is in relationship to the world by which it is constructed'. And that there is, therefore, a basis for ethical discussion.

This problematic position of the subject, and of ethical engagement in the world, is also clearly perceptible in feminist theories. Addressing feminism as separatism, as difference and as discourse theory, Soper reveals that autonomy is not the easiest of concepts for feminism to address (see the accusations that de Beauvoir is adopting patriarchal ideology in her stress on independence). Yet humanism, an assertion of sameness, is equally problematic for the 'difference feminists', Irigaray and Cixous, who seem to rule out the possibility of male–female dialogue implicit in de Beauvoir's demand to reconciliation and integration. An alternative to these feminist positions is found in current reworkings of Marxist theory. Habermas, the avowedly modernist critic of postmodernism, offers a critique of instrumental rationality which has much to offer feminist critiques of patriarchal knowledge and power structures. This form of feminist theory provides an alternative to all those feminists who were driven, through dissatisfaction with orthodox Marxism's gender-blindness to post-structuralism, to Lacanian psychoanalysis, Levi-Strauss's kinship theory, Foucauldian and Derridean 'culturalism'. As Soper states: 'a gender-sensitized Habermasian theory ... must be thought to provide a promising alternative to the Hobson's choice between unreconstructed Marxism, and structuralism/post-structuralist fatalism and nihilism.' What Kate Soper advocates in its place is a two-pronged strategy: the assertion of in-difference and rejection of essentializing discourses, and the retention of the category of 'woman' as a practical political strategy. What we need, claims Soper, is both a humanist and feminist political and moral commitment.

This, I fully accept, may sound to some less like a theoretical grounding that a series of, possibly incompatible, critiques and quibbles. But I, for one, found in this collection a refreshingly coherent concern with issues too long neglected, too frequently marginalized, by the dominant theoretical debates of the day. To assert the importance of morality, of need, of agency, and to place these issues in the context of the array of competing theoretical agendas currently vying for recognition is an illuminating project. It is a brave and difficult position to adopt. Brave because it is open to criticism and scepticism from both the Marxist and the postmodern camps of thought. And difficult because it attempts to salvage elements of each in an, as yet, slightly troubled whole. But this project is motivated less by a desire for theoretical consistency than for the provision of a framework which will enable us to act, to engage with the world in a practical and helpful manner.

And it is perhaps due to this motivation that Soper finds herself feeling ambivalent about theory itself. In this collection she combines essays, reviews, pieces of criticism and fiction. Each with different specific objects of concern, but all with the same fundamental underlying agenda. What gradually emerges is a humanist concern with need and how to satisfy its various manifestations, how to realize the conditions of human flourishing. And there is much to be said for approaching this from different angles, in different genres. For while theoretical work demands a certain form of precision, a clear coherent line of thought, fictional pieces can address issues, play with them, explore their implications, without having a conclusion in mind: one can raise questions without having answers. To cross these disciplinary boundaries; to allow ourselves to write, and therefore to think, in different forms can only help us break through restricting theoretical constraints; allowing ourselves to be open to the implicit illumination of an idea, rather than its explicit evaluation.

It is a joy to find someone rejecting the totalizing solutions offered by the left, while avoiding the nihilistic tendency of postmodernism to opt out of political discourse and action altogether. The voguish indifference to values which has come to dominate theoretical writings in recent years is here firmly rejected in favour of an avowedly ethical concern with social relations.

Judith Squires

Conflicts in Feminism
Edited by Marianne Hirsch and
Evelyn Fox Keller
Routledge: London, 1991
ISBN 0 4159 0178 2, £12.99 Pbk

In *Conflicts in Feminism*, Hirsch and
Fox Keller have cast a wide net to
catch the many dimensions of contemporary feminist theory with
topics ranging from race, law, sexuality and writing, to science and
conceptive technologies. Their brief
to contributors was to map out
feminist debates in each field most of
which focus on the equality/differ-
ence battle (whether women need
the same or different treatment from
men). I was eager to review this
book. At last, I thought, a book addressing the most critically urgent
issues in contemporary feminism
which will have feminist answers to
the even more critically urgent
issues of race and gender inequalities and sexual violence. The anthology bears witness to the deeply
felt need of feminists today to understand how we see and hear each
other's differences historically,
sociologically and in writing. It contains Sara Ruddick's fascinating
development of her 'maternal thinking' theory (the idea that positive
social and ethical practices emerge
from mothering roles) to a novel
'labour theory' of gender-inclusive
mothering.

The volume is itself a very good
example of process as practice with
its vivid *femmes de lettres* or dialogues between feminist friends such
as Jane Gallop and Nancy Miller.
Feminist theory has revolutionized
the *belles lettres* form, as for example
with Audre Lorde's 'Letter to Mary
Daly'. In a cross-race dialogue between bell hooks and Mary Childers,
hooks resonately points out that the
important question is not whether or
not the white people who invented
psychoanalysis can be blamed for
avoiding the category of race but
rather that white people did not

'invent' psychoanalysis in the first
place. Processes now characterized
as psychoanalytic are to be found
throughout world cultures.

In some ways these dialogues
resemble what in American teaching
are called 'discharge exercises' and
inevitably risk the solipsisms of that
form. For example, Childers' touch-
stone – working-class women's 'direct speaking' – and Ann Snitow's
desperate search for politically vanguard groups betray a fallacious belief in 'true' experience. The equality/
difference theme, how the ideology of
gender differences obscures the variety of women's experiences, is
treated with great care in many
essays. For example, Martha Minow,
with deft candour, delineates feminist disagreements about pornography and maternity-leave policies and
Joan Scott argues convincingly, in
her analysis of the Sears case, that
differences are the very *meaning* of
equality. As with any edited collection some essays will lack the scale of
the enterprise. King-Kok Cheung's
analysis of *The Woman Warrior*
(Kingston, 1977) could have appeared in any text at any time. This
is not to decry Cheung's work but
perhaps to hint at how nonwhite
concerns are not finally central to the
volume.

Which is why the subtle essay by
Teresa de Lauretis arguing that
what is essential (*sic*) to feminism is
not its *properties*, but the *relation* of
its properties, is important. De
Lauretis argues that we should look
at the relations and forms as much as
at the content of feminist political
practices and conceptual elaborat-
ions. This is a significant flyer adver-
tising what could be a feminist mara-
thon. I would love to shadow de
Lauretis situating Asian and Black
feminisms against British government policies as Amina Mama and
others have begun to do (Mama,
1984).

Only two essays fully answer de
Lauretis's call. Valerie Smith makes

an insightful exploration of the interrelated discourses of rape. By including media and fiction along with first-hand accounts she emphatically illustrates one of the key features of feminist theory which is the value of interdisciplinary work. The second essay is Marnia Lazreg's extensive critique of the political frameworks of Western sociology/ anthropology and feminist writing about Algerian women. This is a feminist version of Edward Said's *Orientalism* with the same path-breaking intent. So that it is very odd that only these essays are singled out by the editors in conclusion as those unable to 'break through the silence'. One clue to this lies elsewhere in the pronouns where women of colour are often 'them' (or usually 'they/it') versus 'our', presumably white, feminists. American feminism is still too concerned with changing the signature (academic allegiance) rather than changing the subject (to pun on a phrase in Miller's essay) – the 'yes that's me' response to new represen-

tations of women. Yes I can be a postmodernist, poststructuralist, post anything because I am in post (tenured). What changing the feminist subject would involve, it seems to me, is defining the 'relation' between feminist theory and ethnicities. What can feminist theory say which can undermine racist/nationalist models? What is the interrelatedness of language, social details and womanhood in terms of the exploitation of different ethnic women? But the questions *Conflicts in Feminism* addresses and those that the volume provokes *are* important and together give us a large and dynamic feminist agenda.

Maggie Humm

References

KINGSTON, Maxine Hong (1977) *The Woman Warrior* New York: Vintage Press.
MAMA, Amina (1984) 'Black women, the economic crisis, and the British state' in *Feminist Review* No 17.

Feminist Interpretations and Political Theory
Edited by Mary Lyndon Shanley and Carole Pateman
Polity Press: Cambridge, 1990
ISBN 0 7456 0704 7 £39.50 Hbk;
ISBN 0 7456 0705 5 £10.95 Pbk

Justice, Gender and the Family
Susan Moller Okin
Basic Books: New York, 1989
ISBN 0 4650 3702 $19.95

Feminist political theory has only recently come into its own, for while feminists have been developing their powerful critiques of 'malestream' political thought for many years now, the audience has hitherto been restricted to those grappling with

academic conventions. In the broader context of the contemporary women's movement, the issues that dominated discussion related primarily to the causes of women's oppression: was it capitalism or patriarchy? was it economics or ideology? was it structures or prejudices or roles? These were key preoccupations in the first decades of contemporary feminism, and they gave special prominence to the insights of women working in the areas of economics, sociology, anthropology or history. Those working in the field of political theory were cast in a more limited and supporting role.

Through most of the 1960s and 1970s, political theory remained pretty impervious to any of feminism's concerns. Theory courses never included women writers; rarely bothered to mention texts where the great men had ventured their opinions on relations between the sexes; and almost invariably concealed the wealth of spoken and unspoken assumptions that political theorists made about women and men. Works like Susan Moller Okin's earlier *Women in Western Political Thought* (1979) began to correct this imbalance, and for those who had been taken through the standard course in political theorists, provided much needed and welcome illumination. The two books that are the subject of this review continue and develop this work, and between them cover virtually the entire canon of contemporary and classical theory. They will be read with particular excitement by anyone embattled on this terrain, but the issues they raise now relate more directly to what have become central feminist concerns. The increasing importance attached to the tension between equality and difference combines with the growing interest around questions of citizenship, democracy and justice, to make feminist political theory much more the flavour of the day.

The collection edited by Mary Shanley and Carole Pateman is a really fine compilation of recently published or newly commissioned essays, covering the conventional and not so conventional canon. The writers dealt with range from Plato and Aristotle to Hegel, Foucault, Habermas and de Beauvoir; they include feminists who are usually omitted from discussions of political theory; and political theorists who had previously escaped such detailed feminist critique. Linking all (fourteen) contributions is a shared belief that arguments about women and men have been fundamental, if all too often implicit, in the development of political thought. In sustained and critical analysis, the essays reveal the continuing consequences of the separation between public and private domains, and the way this has worked to

obscure or reinforce women's relative exclusion. For those who might have considered this an earlier aberration, the essays on Arendt or Habermas or Rawls demonstrate the more sorry truth of contemporary thinking: that, after centuries of feminist argument and campaigning, the gender subtext still works to keep women out.

If this suggests that the collection is no more than variations on a single theme – applying to each theorist in succession what is basically the same critique – nothing could be more misleading. For despite their shared starting point, the contributors then divide up between two increasingly clearly defined positions. Women were not automatically included within the apparently universal scope of citizenship, rights, freedom or equality; and for some of those represented here, the crucial failing of previous political theory was precisely this deviation from the supposedly universal into a more gender-specific – that is, masculine – set of concerns. From this perspective, the problem is how to push political theory into living up to its own ideals, so that citizenship or justice can at last become genuinely gender-neutral. Others in this volume, however, see the very ideal of a unitary model as potentially fraudulent – and readers of *The Sexual Contract* will already know Carole Pateman as a major contributor to this view. From this second perspective, sexual differentiation is not something that can be readily erased from political theory, but should be consciously and explicitly written in. The question of what difference sexual difference should make has of course become central to feminist argument, and this collection of essays has a great deal to offer in furthering these debates.

The essay on Rawls is extracted from Susan Moller Okin's *Justice, Gender and the Family*, which takes on the leading lights on the contemporary political stage: John Rawls,

Michael Sandel, Robert Nozick, Alasdair MacIntyre, Michael Walzer, Robert Unger. Okin is one of the most powerful voices in the argument for gender-neutrality, and the object of her attack is what she sees as *falsely* gender-neutral approaches. Feminism has had enough of an impact to alter at least the language of political theorists. The change has been more marked in the USA than in Britain, but many now replace their masculine pronouns with 'he or she'; some, like Richard Rorty, have switched to using 'she' throughout; while others get their computers to distribute the 'he' and 'she' randomly through their text. As Okin notes, this has some odd consequences – as when people discuss abortion and pregnancy as matters for people of indifferent sex.

I shall not attempt to summarize the wealth of argument she develops in her examination of contemporary political thinking, but will concentrate on the underlying perspective which illuminates her work. Okin envisages a world in which 'the deeply entrenched institutionalization of sexual difference' (this is her definition of gender) is reduced to its minimum: a world in whose 'social structures and practices, one's sex would have no more relevance than one's eye colour or the length of one's toes' (171). Because of the importance she attaches to impartial justice, she sees a Rawlsian liberalism as providing the basic groundwork for this: once extended and revised to cover the family and the sexual division of labour (which Rawls simply assumed to be just) she sees the notion of justice as fairness and impartiality as offering real potential for challenging the inequalities of gender. Okin's approach thus cuts across the extensive debates within North American feminism on the contrasting ethics of justice (male) and care (female); and explicitly warns against the waste of feminist energy in trying to show that 'justice' is an essentially masculinist moral-

ity. The problem with contemporary political theory lies not so much in the versions it offers of morality or justice, as in the recurrent exclusion of the family as somehow outside their scope.

I have considerable sympathy with this argument, and of the two broadly defined schools of thought that are represented in the Shanley and Pateman collection, find myself increasingly drawn towards those that emphasize the possibility of gender-neutral standards of justice. I would gladly do without most of what currently passes for sexual difference; and if orthodox theorists have erred on the side of writing masculinity into their seemingly gender-free categories, I would not want to compound this by writing in some version of femininity instead. But as I travel from the abstractions of equality to the specificities of difference and then back to universal aspirations once again, I am caught up short by the poverty of Susan Moller Okin's conclusions.

Shared parenting is at the heart of her proposals for reducing the gender-structuring of marriage and the family, but given the huge numbers of single – especially divorced – parents in the USA, she recognizes that this barely touches the needs of the most vulnerable groups. A crucial additional policy is then for the absent fathers to pay more money. In particular, she suggests, the terms of divorce settlement should be drawn up so as to guarantee that both post-divorce households can enjoy the same standard of living; this would contrast sharply to current US experience, where divorce typically brings severe poverty to the ex-wife. But in the context of recent British debates on chasing up recalcitrant fathers and getting them to pay more for the support of each child, Susan Moller Okin's proposals have a very odd ring. She does not explore the possibilities of providing child support through the state rather than the individual; she does not consider the position of those women who may for very good reasons want nothing more to do with the father of their children; she does not explore the way that paying money makes people feel they have a right to intervene. With all the power of her critique of orthodox theory, she retains a strangely benign – and ultimately individualist – view of sexual relations.

How much of this can be attributed to her underlying theoretical perspective: her sense of gender difference as the problem, which in the name of justice must be substantially reduced? I would not want to attach too much significance to the poverty of her policy conclusions: anyone who has written feminist theory will know the pressure to follow through with practical implications, and the risks of then adding on a relatively underdeveloped policy review. But the failure to engage with the more bitter and brutal aspects of male-female re-lations does seem to connect with the fundamentally liberal perception of unfairness and inequality as the problem. If so, then it may reinforce the case of those feminists (a number of whom are represented in the Shanley and Pateman collection) who see the very notion of gender-neutrality as already weighted in the interests of the male.

These are issues that will continue to preoccupy feminist theory and debate, and I recommend both books highly for the way they pursue and clarify such concerns. Both texts will find a ready and enthusiastic audience among those engaged more directly with political theory. But their potential readership now reaches beyond the academic confines, and both have a great deal to say to anyone grappling with current feminist debates. Both are also a very good read.

Anne Phillips

Women and Disability
Susan Lonsdale
Macmillan: London, 1990
ISBN 0 3334 2666 5 £8.99 Pbk

One only needs to browse through feminist literature to realize the extent to which disabled women have remained absent, or on the periphery of feminist discussions. Therefore it was with great enthusism that I took the opportunity to review *Women and Disability*.

The book is structured in a fairly familiar academic format. Susan Lonsdale starts with a review of existing literature which incorporates a discussion of the prevalence of disability and considers the social context of disability. It then goes on to look at how disabled women have been rendered invisible by both pro-fessional service providers and society at large. This provides a backdrop to chapters on self-image and sexuality, and dependency.

The use of a small-scale study helps to demonstrate how disabled women have to confront the same issues as other women, but often do not have access to the same basic rights. For example, Lonsdale cites the experiences of one disabled woman who attended a residential school: 'I wanted privacy, especially when I first started having my periods. I was fifteen and the youngest was six. You got washed in front of all of them. And you had your period pads changed in front of them. I learned about periods from what I had seen when I was younger.' (91)

The author touches upon certain themes which have been central to understanding women's experiences. The discussion appears sometimes to be somewhat superficial; there is a tendency to gloss over or avoid particular issues. For example, disabled lesbians only warrant a fleeting mention and there is no analysis of the particular issues faced by them.

Lonsdale places her analysis in a policy framework by providing a clear and comprehensive examination of the impact of employment and financial policies on the lives of disabled women. This is the most useful and informative part of the book, particularly as the author goes on to discuss how disabled women are not protected by antidiscrimination and civil rights policies. The book concludes by examining policies and practices which should offer disabled women a greater degree of self-determination and independence.

The author interviewed twenty-two disabled women 'of different ages, races and socio-economic backgrounds', but their views and experiences only appear in the context of supporting or demonstrating her points. The research material could have played a crucial role in bringing the voices of disabled women to the forefront but, unfortunately, it appears that the demands of academia prevailed and the women interviewed were silenced.

Lonsdale claims 'all the black women interviewed said that their disability was a greater handicap than their colour' (45) I am somewhat alarmed at the assumption that the dimensions of race and disability can be isolated and pitched against one another. I can't recall Lonsdale reporting whether the white women she interviewed thought disability was a greater handicap than their gender. It is the cumulative influences of being black, disabled and female which shape our lives. To suggest that any of these factors can be ranked in a hierarchical order is a dangerous road to go down.

Susan Lonsdale's book has arrived in a field where there is an urgent need for discussion and debate. However, as a disabled woman reading this book, I cannot help but feel uncomfortable and disappointed. The author states that she has an interest and commitment to addressing the experiences of disabled women. This I do not doubt. However, when a nondisabled woman starts writing about disabled women without addressing her position, or stating what personal and professional perspectives she brings to the research, then I do have serious cause for concern.

Interestingly, Lonsdale writes: 'Very little attention has been devoted to the situation of women who are disabled, and what does exist has usually been written by the women themselves' (40). I trust Ms Lonsdale is not attempting to dismiss disabled women's writing and, I hope she is not implying that our work is not worthy of the same recognition as other academic writing. As disabled women writers we are fighting for the right to be recognized and accepted as equals in both mainstream and feminist circles. Lonsdale (and other feminist academics) must take positive steps to develop a working relationship with us. They should focus their time and energy on enabling us to document our experiences instead of writing on our behalf.

Feminism has now recognized that white women cannot write about the experiences of black women without it being problematical. Similarly, nondisabled women must question their ability to develop an analysis of our experiences as disabled women without it being problematical.

One of the major obstacles facing disabled women is the attitudes of nondisabled people. It's a pity that Susan Lonsdale, as a nondisabled author, did not take the opportunity to explore the experiences of nondisabled people (particularly women) when interacting with disabled people (especially women).

There is an urgent need for a discussion about disabled women's relationships with the women's movement and how the two interact. Towards the end of the book Lonsdale points out: 'In many ways, the objectives of the women's movement and groups of disabled women are the same: ending discrimination, developing a consciousness among women of how they are disadvantaged, and attempting to reshape and restructure society along feminist lines. But . . . some of the symbols of combating oppression which the women's movement adopted, such as abortion on demand and a rejection of excessive femininity, have often been considered unacceptable to women with disabilities because they gloss over issues which are crucial to them.' (161)

Disabled women are an integral part of the women's movement, therefore the women's movement must reflect our needs, wishes and aspirations. It is unfortunate that Lonsdale did not explore the issues further by airing some of the debates more thoroughly.

Women and Disability is useful in terms of providing a comprehensive analysis of disability policies and the impact of these on disabled women. But in terms of providing a thorough analysis of the experiences of disabled women the reader is short-changed. In a field where there is very little written material available, one must be wary of treating it as an authoritative text. Our voices as disabled women are only heard through the mouthpiece of a nondisabled woman. This must make the reader question whether the written text really does justice to our experiences as disabled women.

Nasa Begum

Issues of Blood: The Politics of Menstruation

Sophie Laws

Macmillan: London, 1990
ISBN 0 333 48234 4 £9.99 Pbk;
ISBN 0 333 48233 6 £35.00 Hbk

Most of the feminist work concerned with menstruation has come from the matriarchalist/essentialist radical-feminist schools of thought (Weideger, 1978; Delaney, Lupton and Toth, 1976; Shuttle and Redgrove, 1978). Sophie Laws's painstaking investigation into the politics of menstruation is a self-conscious exercise in developing a social-constructionist and yet radical-feminist perspective which refutes biological determinist and universalist explanations. She seeks instead to describe and make sense of social meanings and explore the ways in which competing social definitions interact. Looking at the social treatment of menstruation and how the practices of our own culture spell out messages about male superiority and compulsory heterosexuality to women, Laws argues that in a patriarchal society, menstruation is seen by men as a marker of femaleness and used to convey a particular belief in women's inferior status.

In order to present a social constructionist argument, Laws's first task was to challenge the universal menstrual taboo theory of much anthropological research in this area. The taboo theory proposes that menstrual blood is inherently dirty and that men are naturally repulsed by a physical function they do not share with women. Laws goes to great lengths to reveal the existence of an immense variety of cultural practices relating to menstruation and argues that it is not useful to reduce the complexity and variety of ritual, practice and beliefs around menstruation across different cultures to generalized statements about taboos. The tendency of Western male anthropologists to emphasize menstrual taboo says more about their own preoccupations than it reveals about the cultures they have observed.

Rather than the universalist notion of taboos, Laws has identified a menstrual 'etiquette' which operates in contemporary British secular culture. Defined by Laws as 'a set of social practices which express and reinforce the distinctions between people of different social statuses' I found this notion of etiquette useful, although it does not allow for an examination of the role played by religious discourse in constructing widely held beliefs about menstruation. The etiquette requires that women may not make men aware of the existence of menstruation either implicitly or explicitly; those who do are ridiculed, harassed or avoided by men. Many of us will recognize the descriptions cited by Laws of the extraordinary lengths women have gone to in order to conceal the fact that they are bleeding.

Starting with the hypothesis that what men say about menstruation has engendered women's sense of shame, Laws selected to research into what a group of men had to say on the subject, probing especially questions of how they thought they had aquired the attitudes and beliefs they held. This is the type of research very few feminists would choose to undertake as many of us have an idea of the hateful nature of many men's reactions to menstruation. Laws herself found it hard to conceal her distaste for much of what she heard from her subjects. This raised methodological problems for Laws as her lack of empathy with her subjects made deciphering the interviews difficult and she failed to provide a coherent description of their views. Sociologists have tradition-

ally relied greatly on empathy with their research subjects in making their interpretations and Laws is aware that her work lacks this insight. The personal strain of carrying out this research is highlighted repeatedly throughout the text, leaving me wondering whether there wasn't a less traumatic way of obtaining the data.

Laws's distaste for her subjects permeates the text and creates a mood of deep pessimism throughout the book, something much radical-feminist writing manages to do. It would be a shame if this put people off as the book positively bursts with data and insight. I did feel, however, that Laws's discussion of gynaecological discourse on menstruation was far too brief and not related to wider social attitudes. That both gynaecologists and Laws's men believe women imagine or exaggerate menstrual pain was an important discovery, however the relationship between the two discourses was not adequately explored. Laws suggests that as most gynaecologists are men then this is simply an echo of male beliefs about menstruation. Laws sees no need to discuss difference between men, which allows her to see all men as having the same access to power and influence, a position which prevents her from examining the particular power of certain discourses.

The public denial of menstrual pain stands in an interesting contrast to 'premenstrual tension'. That men more readily accept the impact of hormonal fluctuations on women's mood changes rather than believe that we often experience real, sometimes excruciating pain, is evidence of a system of gender stereotyping which clings to the notion that women are essentially irrational, victims of our hormones. The construction of PMT into a diseaselike category has created very negative connotations for women. Thus, in cases of female violence the judiciary will now accept a plea of temporary

insanity by virtue of hormonal fluctuations, yet doggedly resist
women's pleas of provocation even in
the most horrific cases of domestic
violence. The brutality experienced
by some women at the hands of men
they live with still goes unacknowledged within legal discourse while
PMT is eagerly embraced as con-
firmation of women's biologically determined emotional instability.
Laws argues convincingly that in
this case the dismantling of menstrual etiquette has not necessarily
been liberatory.

Menstruation may not be important in itself, but it is highly
symbolic of femaleness and the ways
in which men deal with it reveal
aspects of how they view women in
general. The main problem with
Laws's analysis is her monolithic
view of male power, unmediated by
considerations of class, race or age.
When I first read this book, I was left
with the same sense of hopelessness
and exasperation which permeates
the text. However, on a closer reading and Laws's pessimism notwith-
standing, I discovered that it does
contain some cause for optimism
which is not acknowledged by the
author.

It was evident from what some
of the men had told Laws that some
women do indeed act within their
relationships to challenge men's pre-
conceived and misogynist ideas
about women's bodies; some women
are refusing to hide the fact of their
menstruation from men they know

or live with; some women are actively seeking sex with men while
menstruating because *they* experience heightened desire at this time;
and some men (albeit only a few from
this small sample but surely that is
positive) are concerned to understand more about menstruation and
how women feel about it. It is the
public arena which remains dominated by powerful institutions (law,
medicine) and largely male-only
groupings which remains overtly
hostile to women defining their own
bodily and social experience. It does
not help our understanding of power
in society, who has it and who
benefits from it, to see all men as
members of an oppressive brother-
hood which seeks ultimately to keep
us in our rightful place. Such a position presents women only as passive
recipients of male oppression and is
negative about the possibility of
change. It is crucial, therefore, to
remind women not only of how far we
have to go, as Laws does, but also to
celebrate how far we have come.

Shiona McArthur

References

DELANEY, J., LUPTON, M. J. and TOTH, E.
(1976) *The Curse: A Cultural History of
Menstruation* New York: E. P. Dalton.
SHUTTLE, Penelope and REDGROVE, Peter
(1978) *The Wise Wound: Menstruation
and Everywoman* London: Victor Goll-
ancz; Harmondsworth: Penguin, 1980.
WIEDEGER, Paula (1978) *Female Cycles*
London: Women's Press.

Noticeboard

Call for Submissions: Short Fiction by Women

Submissions are now being accepted for *Short Fiction by Women*, a new magazine publishing the finest literature by women writers. The magazine needs short stories, novellas and novel excerpts. All women writers – published and unpublished – are invited to submit their work.

Payment will be based on length and funds available. The magazine will own first serial rights only. Writers should submit one typed, double-spaced manuscript (in English) and include a SAE for return of manuscript. Send submissions to: Rachel Whalen, Editor, *Short Fiction by Women*, Box 1276, Stuyvesant Station, New York NY 10009 USA.

The first issue will be published in the fall of 1991. Thereafter, publication will be three times a year. Subscriptions are available for $18 per year.

Now Available

'1992 and You' – The Office Workers' Survival Kit for the 1990s

'1992 and You' is an information pack aimed at office workers and their representatives. It looks at the impact of the Single European Market on office jobs and compares working and living conditions across the European Community.

The pack consists of individual factsheets covering Employment; Money; Family; Equality; Health; Legal; Trade Unions plus a useful section on further help and resources.

'1992 and You' is available from City Centre, 32/35 Featherstone Street, London EC1Y 8QX price £4 including postage and packing.

For further information contact Rohan Collier or Irene Hamilton: 071 608 1338

An Pobal Eirithe

The Spring 1991 issue of *An Pobal Eirithe* – the magazine of the Irish in Britain Representation Group (IBRG) includes an eight-page supplement 'A Further Bibliography of the History of the Irish in Britain' with over 350 listings. It is the first such compilation to appear since the publication in 1986 of a bibliography by the now defunct Irish in Britain History Centre and it updates and extends the sources. Copies of the magazine cost £1.20 each including postage and packaging and you should send a cheque or postal order made payable to IBRG c/o Hornsey Library, Haringey Park, Crouch End, London N8. A report on the IBRG national education conference. 'Irish Perspective on British Education' is also available, price £1.00 from the same address.

The Private Case

The Private Case offers a mail-order catalogue of books about sexual pleasure and politics, the erotic in art and literature, children's and adolescent sexuality. The Private Case works closely with the Sexuality Library in San Francisco, which was begun by a woman sex educator and therapist who had been publishing a number of sexual self-help books. It is now part of a thriving business run by thirteen women, all of whom share the philosophy that everyone is entitled to a healthy and happy sex life. For more information and a catalogue write to:
The Private Case, P.O. Box 1632, London N15 4LG.

Call For Papers

Lancaster Women's Studies One-Day Conference

The second Lancaster Women's Studies Annual Conference will take place on Saturday 21 March 1992. Papers and workshops have been invited on the subject of 'Romance Revisited'.

Plenary Speakers include: Bridget Fowler (Glasgow University); Stevi Jackson (Polytechnic of Wales); Alison Light (University of London); Helen Taylor (University of Warwick).

This will be an interdisciplinary conference and we welcome proposals on topics such as: theories of romance/romantic love; visual/literary representations of romance; romance, marriage and 'the family'; lesbian and gay romance; romance and gender identity; heterosexuality and romance; possession, jealousy and revenge; romance and ethnic/national identity; desire and sexuality; romance and legal discourses; romantic love and sexual violence; psychoanalytic perspectives on romance; romance and class differences; youth cultures and romance; 'happy endings'.

For further details write to: Lynne Pearce and Jackie Stacey, Centre for Women's Studies, Lancaster University, Lancaster (tel. 0524 65201, ext. 2234 or ext. 4171).

First International Conference on Girls and Girlhood – Advance Announcement

'Alice in Wonderland: Girls and Girlhood: Transitions and Dilemmas' will be the first international academic conference exclusively devoted to girls. One objective is to trace the extent and diversity of the scattered research being done; a further aim is to locate and discuss the social policies and ideological strategies by means of which 'girls' are defined and situated in society. 'Alice in Wonderland' intends to call into question the seemingly unproblematical equation of socio-political questions and the historical beings called girls. Girls, girlhood and girlishness are socio-historically and ideologically determined notions, and as such, subject to change. The programme consists of plenary lectures and six sections of papers: Eros, Sexuality and the Body; Policy-Making and the State; Imagination and Representation; Education and Upbringing; Youth Culture and Life-World; Employment and Schooling; Theory and Epistemology.

It will be held at the University of Amsterdam, 16–19 June 1992. For further information and offers of papers, write to 'Alice in Wonderland', First International Conference on Girls and Girlhood, Conference Service Vrije Universiteit, De Boelelaan 1105, 1081 HV Amsterdam, The Netherlands.

Women Living Under Muslim Laws Network

Please note that the contact address for this organization given on page 102 of *Feminist Review* No. 37 was incorrect and women wishing to contact the network should write to: WLUML, BP 23, 34790, Grabels, France; or telephone 67 45 43 29.

We apologize to the network for this error.

A New Lesbian and Gay Film and Video Archive and Home Video Service

Albany Video Distribution is launching a new non-profitmaking company – OUT On A Limb to promote the distribution of Lesbian and Gay films and videos.

OUT On A Limb's home video service will, initially, operate on a mail-order basis. In time, however, we intend to distribute the work of lesbian and gay film-makers through high-street retail outlets. The few mainstream lesbian or gay films to be produced – *Desert Hearts*, *Longtime Companion* and *Torch Song Trilogy*, for example – are currently available on video but they may not always be stocked by the corner video shop. OUT On A Limb aims to encourage mainstream distributors to promote lesbian and gay work as energetically as they would any other.

At the same time, OUT On A Limb will operate as a national archive for lesbian and gay work past and present. OUT On A Limb will, therefore, be a unique and invaluable resource.

Sponsorship
Although we intend OUT On A Limb to become fully self-financing, we are initially seeking individual and business sponsorship to cover start-up costs. We are looking for one-off donations; regular contributions to our costs, by way of a bank standing order for example; and the offer of services in kind. In return, as a sponsor of OUT On A Limb you will be entitled to reduced subscription rates to our Home Video service; invitations to all screenings, including premières of new work; and inclusion on our mailing list (we hope to be able to keep sponsors in touch by way of a regular newsletter).

We expect our start-up costs to be in the region of £10,000. We need to cover the costs of (at least) the following items:

- A paid worker
- A computer system to cope with the demands of a new business
- The design of a corporate image and company logo, the printing of new stationery and promotional material and the packaging of videos
- Advertising and promotion
- Conversion of videos from American (NTSC) to British (PAL) format and of films to video
- Certification of videos

If you can help we want to hear from you. You will be helping to set up a unique and invaluable resource which will ensure the documentation of an important part of the culture and history of lesbians and gay men; which will promote the work of lesbian and gay film- and video-makers to wider audiences at home and abroad; and which may in time lead to the establishment of an independent production company dedicated to supporting and financing new work by lesbian and gay film- and video-makers. With trade barriers within the European Community due to come down in 1992, there are excellent new opportunities for the distribution and exhibition of lesbian and gay work. OUT On A Limb, the only such company in Europe, is ideally placed to take advantage of them.

OUT On A Limb, Battersea Studios, Television Centre, Thackeray Road, London SW8 3TW
Tel: 071-498 9643 Fax: 071-498 1494
OUT On A Limb Ltd is registered in England and Wales, company No. 2613707

✂············**CUT HERE**···

I/We would like to sponsor **OUT On A Limb** and (please tick appropriate box)

☐   I/We enclose a donation of £_____ (cheques/POs to: **OUT On A Limb**)

☐   I/We can provide services in kind (details enclosed)

☐   I/We would like to contribute on a regular basis. Please send details.

☐   I/We would like to become business sponsors. Please send details.

NAME_____   **COMPANY**_____

ADDRESS_____

_____   **PHONE**_____

Now please send this form to the address given above. Thank You.

Feminist Review

Since its founding in 1979 **Feminist Review** has been the major Women's Studies journal in Britain. **Feminist Review** is committed to presenting the best of contemporary feminist analysis, always informed by an awareness of changing political issues. The journal is edited by a collective of women based in London, with the help of women and groups from all over the United Kingdom.

● WHY NOT SUBSCRIBE? MAKE SURE OF YOUR COPY

All subscriptions run in calendar years. The issues for 1992 are Nos. 40, 41 and 42. You will save over £6 pa on the single copy price.

● SUBSCRIPTION RATES, 1992 (3 issues)

Individual Subscriptions

UK/EEC	£21.00
Overseas	£28
North America	$46

A number of reduced cost (£15.50 per year: UK only) subscriptions are available for readers experiencing financial hardship, e.g. unemployed, student, low-paid. If you'd like to be considered for a reduced subscription, please write to the Collective, c/o the Feminist Review office

Institutional Subscriptions		**Back Issues**	
UK	£50	UK	£8.99
Overseas	£55	North America	$16.50
North America	$90		

☐ Please send me one year's subscription to **Feminist Review**

☐ Please send me⎯⎯⎯⎯⎯copies of back issue no.⎯⎯⎯⎯

METHOD OF PAYMENT

☐ I enclose a cheque/international money order to the value of⎯⎯⎯⎯⎯⎯⎯
made payable to Routledge Journals

☐ Please charge my Access/Visa/American Express/Diners Club account

Account no. ☐☐☐☐☐☐☐☐☐☐☐☐☐☐☐☐☐☐

Expiry date⎯⎯⎯⎯⎯⎯⎯⎯⎯⎯⎯ Signature⎯⎯⎯⎯⎯⎯⎯⎯⎯⎯

If the address below is different from the registered address of your credit card, please give your registered address separately.

PLEASE USE BLOCK CAPITALS

Name⎯⎯⎯⎯⎯⎯⎯⎯⎯⎯⎯⎯⎯⎯⎯⎯⎯⎯⎯⎯⎯⎯

Address⎯⎯⎯⎯⎯⎯⎯⎯⎯⎯⎯⎯⎯⎯⎯⎯⎯⎯⎯⎯

⎯⎯⎯⎯⎯⎯⎯⎯⎯⎯Postcode⎯⎯⎯⎯⎯⎯⎯⎯⎯

☐ Please send me a Routledge Journals Catalogue

☐ Please send me a Routledge Gender and Women's Studies Catalogue

Please return this form with payment to:
Sharon McDuell, Routledge, 11 New Fetter Lane, London EC4P 4EE

BACK ISSUES

28 FAMILY SECRETS: CHILD SEXUAL ABUSE: Introduction to an Issue: Family Secrets as Public Drama, **McIntosh**. Challenging the Orthodoxy: Towards a Feminist Theory and Practice, **MacLeod & Saraga**. The Politics of Child Sexual Abuse: Notes from American History, **Gordon**. What's in a Name?: Defining Child Sexual Abuse, **Kelly**. A Case, **Anon**. Defending Innocence: Ideologies of Childhood, **Kitzinger**. Feminism and the Seductiveness of the 'Real Event', **Scott**. Cleveland and the Press: Outrage and Anxiety in the Reporting of Child Sexual Abuse, **Nava**. Child Sexual Abuse and the Law, **Woodcraft**. Poem, **Betcher**. Brixton Black Women's Centre: Organizing on Child Sexual Abuse, **Bogle**. Bridging the Gap: Glasgow Women's Support Project, **Bell & Macleod**. Claiming Our Status as Experts: Community Organizing, **Norwich Consultants on Sexual Violence**. Islington Social Services: Developing a Policy on Child Sexual Abuse, **Boushel & Noakes**. Developing a Feminist School Policy on Child Sexual Abuse, **O'Hara**. 'Putting Ideas into their Heads': Advising the Young, **Mills**. Child Sexual Abuse Crisis Lines: Advice for Our British Readers.

29 ABORTION: THE INTERNATIONAL AGENDA: Whatever Happened to 'A Woman's Right to Choose'?, **Berer**. More than 'A Woman's Right to Choose'?, **Himmelweit**. Abortion in the Republic of Ireland, **Barry**. Across the Water, **Irish Women's Abortion Support Group**. Spanish Women and the Alton Bill, **Spanish Women's Abortion Support Group**. The Politics of Abortion in Australia: Freedom, Church and State, **Coleman**. Abortion in Hungary, **Szalai**. Women and Population Control in China: Issues of Sexuality, Power and Control, **Hillier**. The Politics of Abortion in Nicaragua: Revolutionary Pragmatism – or Feminism in the Realm of Necessity?, **Molyneux**. Who Will Sing for Theresa?, **Bernstein**. She's Gotta Have It: The Representation of Black Female Sexuality on Film, **Simmonds**. Poems, **Gallagher**. Dyketactics for Difficult Times: A Review of the 'Homosexuality, Which Homosexuality?' Conference, **Franklin & Stacey**

30 Capital, Gender and Skill: Women Homeworkers in Rural Spain, **Lever**. Fact and Fiction: George Egerton and Nellie Shaw, **Butler**. Feminist Political Organization in Iceland: Some Reflections on the Experience of Kwenna Frambothid, **Dominelli & Jonsdottir**. Under Western Eyes: Feminist Scholarship and Colonial Discourses, **Talpade Mohanty**. Bedroom Horror: The Fatal Attraction of *Intercourse*, **Merck**. AIDS: Lessons from the Gay Community, **Patton**. Poems, **Agbabi**.

31 **THE PAST BEFORE US: 20 YEARS OF FEMINISM:** Slow Change or No Change?: Feminism, Socialism and the Problem of Men, **Segal**. There's No Place Like Home: On the Place of Identity in Feminist Politics, **Adams**. New Alliances: Socialist-Feminism in the Eighties, **Harriss**. Other Kinds of Dreams, **Parmar**. Complexity, Activism, Optimism: Interview with **Angela Y. Davis**. To Be or Not To Be: The Dilemmas of Mothering, **Rowbotham**. Seizing Time and Making New: Feminist Criticism, Politics and Contemporary Feminist Fiction, **Lauret**. Lessons from the Women's Movement in Europe, **Haug**. Women in Management, **Coyle**. Sex in the Summer of '88, **Ardill & O'Sullivan**. Younger Women and Feminism, **Hobsbawm & Macpherson**. Older Women and Feminism, **Stacey; Curtis; Summerskill**.

32 'Those Who Die for Life Cannot Be Called Dead': Women and Human Rights Protest in Latin America, **Schirmer**. Violence Against Black Women: Gender, Race and State Responses, **Mama**. Sex and Race in the Labour Market, **Breugel**. The Dark Continent: Africa as Female Body in Haggard's Adventure Fiction, **Stott**. Gender, Class and the Welfare State: The Case of Income Security in Australia, **Shaver**. Ethnic Feminism: Beyond the Pseudo-Pluralists, **Gorelick**.

33 Restructuring the Woman Question: *Perestroika* and Prostitution, **Waters**. Contemporary Indian Feminism, **Kumar**. 'A Bit On the Side'?: Gender Struggles in South Africa, **Beall, Hassim and Todes**. 'Young Bess': Historical Novels and Growing Up, **Light**. Madeline Pelletier (1874–1939): The Politics of Sexual Oppression, **Mitchell**.

34 **PERVERSE POLITICS: LESBIAN ISSUES**
Pat Parker: A tribute, **Brimstone**. International Lesbianism: Letter from São Paulo, **Rodrigues**; Israel, **Pittsburgh**, Italy, **Fiocchetto**. The De-eroticization of Women's Liberation: Social Purity Movements and the Revolutionary Feminism of Sheila Jeffreys, **Hunt**. Talking About It: Homophobia in the Black Community, **Gomez & Smith**. Lesbianism and the Labour Party, **Tobin**. Skirting the Issue: Lesbian fashion for the 1990s, **Blackman & Perry**. Butch/Femme Obsessions, **Ardill & O'Sullivan**. Archives: The Will to Remember, **Nestle**; International Archives, **Read**. Audre Lorde: Vignettes and Mental Conversations, **Lewis**. Lesbian Tradition, **Field**. Mapping: Lesbians, AIDS and Sexuality An interview with Cindy Patton, **O'Sullivan**. Significant Others: Lesbians and Psychoanalytic Theory, **Hamer**. The Pleasure Threshold: Looking at Lesbian Pornography on Film, **Smyth**. Cartoon, **Charlesworth**. Voyages of the Valkyries: Recent Lesbian Pornographic Writing, **Dunn**.

35 Campaign Against Pornography, **Norden**. The Mothers' Manifesto and Disputes over 'Mutterlichkeit', **Chamberlayne**. Multiple Mediations: Feminist Scholarship in the Age of Multi-National Reception, **Mani**. Cagney and Lacey Revisited, **Alcock & Robson**. Cutting a Dash: The Dress of Radclyffe Hall and Una Troubridge, **Rolley**. Deviant Dress, **Wilson**. The House that Jill Built: Lesbian Feminist Organizing in Toronto, 1976–1980, **Ross**. Women in Professional Engineering: the Interaction of Gendered Structures and Values, **Carter & Kirkup**. Identity Politics and the Hierarchy of Oppression, **Briskin**. Poetry: **Bufkin, Zumwalt**.

36 'The Trouble Is It's Ahistorical': The Problem of the Unconscious in Modern Feminist Theory, **Minsky**. Feminism and Pornography, **Ellis, O'Dair Tallmer**. Who Watches the Watchwomen? Feminists Against Censorship, **Rodgerson & Semple**. Pornography and Violence: What the 'Experts' Really Say, **Segal**. The Woman In My Life: Photography of Women, **Nava**. Splintered Sisterhood: Antiracism in a Young Women's Project, **Connolly**. Woman, Native, Other, **Parmar** interviews **Trinh T. Minh-ha**. Out But Not Down: Lesbians' Experience of Housing, **Edgerton**. Poems: **Evans Davies, Toth, Weinbaum**. Oxford Twenty Years On: Where Are We Now?, **Gamman & O'Neill**. The Embodiment of Ugliness and the Logic of Love: The Danish Redstockings Movement, **Walter**.

37   THEME ISSUE: WOMEN, RELIGION AND DISSENT
Black Women, Sexism and Racism: Black or Antiracist Feminism?, **Tang Nain**.
Nursing Histories: Reviving Life in Abandoned Selves, **McMahon**. The Quest for
National Identity: Women, Islam and the State in Bangladesh, **Kabeer**. Born
Again Moon: Fundamentalism in Christianity and the Feminist Spirituality
Movement, **McCrickard**. Washing our Linen: One Year of Women Against
Fundamentalism, **Connolly. Siddiqui** on *Letter to Christendom*, **Bard** on
Generations of Memories, **Patel** on *Women Living Under Muslim Laws Dossiers
1–6*, Poem, **Kay**. More Cagney and Lacey, **Gamman**..

38   The Modernist Style of Susan Sontag, **McRobbie**. Tantalizing Glimpses of Stolen
Glances: Lesbians Take Photographs, **Fraser and Boffin**. Reflections on the
Women's Movement in Trinidad, **Mohammed**. Fashion, Representation and
Femininity, **Evans and Thornton**. The European Women's Lobby, **Hoskyns**.
Hendessi on *Law of Desire: Temporary Marriage in Iran*, **Kaveney** on *Mercy*.

39   SHIFTING TERRITORIES: FEMINISM & EUROPE
Between Hope and Helplessness: Women in the GDR, **Dolling**. Where Have All the
Women Gone? Women and the Women's Movement in East Central Europe,
Einhorn. The End of Socialism in Europe – A New Challenge For Socialist
Feminism? **Haug**. The Second 'No': Women in Hungary, **Kiss**. The Citizenship
Debate: Women, the State and Ethnic Processes, **Yuval-Davis**. Fortress Europe
and Migrant Women, **Morokvasíc**. Racial Equality and 1992, **Dummett**.
Questioning *Perestroika*: A Socialist Feminist Interrogation, **Pearson**.
Postmodernism and its Discontents, **Soper**. **Feminists and Socialism:** After the
Cold War, **Kaldor**. Socialism Out of the Common Pots, **Mitter**. 1989 and All That,
Campbell. In Listening Mode, **Cockburn**. **Women in Action: Country by
Country:** The Soviet Union; Yugoslavia; Czechoslovakia; Hungary; Poland.
Reports: International Gay and Lesbian Association: Black Women and Europe
1992.

Women's Voices, Women's Lives

Lewd Women and Wicked Witches
A Study of the Dynamics of Male Domination
Marianne Hester

Unique insights into the ways men maintain their power over women by using sexual violence and sexual constructions of women subtly as well as overtly.

January 1992: 256pp: Hb: 0-415-07071-6: £35.00: Pb: 0-415-05209-2: £10.99

Regulating Womanhood
Historical Essays on Marriage, Motherhood and Sexuality
Edited by **Carol Smart**

Regulating Womanhood examines the social regulation of women through law during the nineteenth and twentieth centuries, and the resistance which emerged in response.

March 1992: 256pp: Hb: 0-415-06080-X: £35.00: Pb: 0-415-07405-3: £10.99

Young, Female and Black
Heidi Safia Mirza

Young black women symbolise the effects of the inequalities of British society. Heidi Safia Mirza, a black woman sociologist, charts the experience of a group of young black women and investigates why black women suffer injustices.

March 1992: 256pp: Hb: 0-415-06704-9: £35.00: Pb: 0-415-06705-7: £10.99

At the Boundaries of Law
Feminism and Legal Theory
Edited by **Martha A. Fineman** and **Nancy S. Thomadsen**

Focussing on the intersection between feminism and legal theory, *At the Boundaries of Law* offers a refreshing challenge to much of the mainstream thought, literature, and methodology in law and the social sciences.

1991: 368pp: Hb: 0-415-90305-X: £35.00: Pb: 0-415-90306-8: £14.99

Child Care and the Psychology of Development
Elly Singer

Elly Singer's exciting book sheds fresh and critical light on the debates surrounding the provision of child-care. She focusses on what is known of the psychological consequences for both children and parents, setting the debates in their political and historical contexts.

Critical Psychology Series
March 1992: 192pp: Hb: 0-415-05591-1: £30.00: Pb: 0-415-05592-X: £10.99

For further information please contact:

Routledge,
11 New Fetter Lane,
London
EC4P 4EE.
Tel: 071 583 9855

Routledge,
Chapman and Hall Inc.
29 West 35th Street
New York, NY 10001
Tel: 244 3336

ROUTLEDGE